YESTERDAY'S NEWS

YESTERDAY'S NEWS

Taylor Brady

FACTORY SCHOOL

ITHACA / SAN DIEGO / SAN FRANCISCO

2005

YESTERDAY'S NEWS by Taylor Brady

First edition, Factory School 2005

ISBN 0-9711863-8-3

Cover Image: *Yesterday's News*, by Tanya Hollis, mixed media on canvas, 2004. Courtesy of David Robbins and Allison Gorley.

Acknowledgments:
Some of these poems previously appeared, or are forthcoming, in the following publications: *Tripwire 6.5 (RNC/NYC special issue), A Very Small Tiger, VeRT, War & Peace, Mixed-Use* (No Press chapbook, 2004), *Untitled* (split chapbook with Tyrone Williams, A Rest Press, 2003), and as part of Elliot Anderson's *CAMS* installation, Gallery 16, San Francisco, 2004. The author wishes to thank the publishers and curators for their support.

FACTORY SCHOOL
Ithaca / San Diego / San Francisco
factoryschool.org

for Leon Brady

CONTENTS

No one will want to read our poems after the war, and this speculation constitutes our hope and ranks there.

Rob Halpern, *Rumored Place*

THEY STORE IT UP

I think my head is growing a head of its own. When I lay it on things its hole fills up with grass and spent shell casings. From this mulch it brings up numbers that have nothing to do with streets or counting bodies where they sit or lie, for which uses I had it built. Damp creeps into its seams and hinges, more every day, until it swells and oozes with a dim futurity that at best can raise no more than boils to mark the passing of one toxic episode after another. Here with all its unforeseen injunctions is the place you make between your body and a sky filling up with more slow rain to come. Or at least I do, in the first place as a city, and in the second place another city, then later as a faint burnt whiff of something out there. Something inside the satellite map waits to emerge, leaving reasons for invisibility on the front side of my skull.

WITHOUT YOUR ASS

(Sun Ra, "Nuclear War")

Chunky suave.
When everybody knows
you're naked.

Get reinforced knees.
Get swagger stick.
Spit. Get reinforcements

to pump the ground
before the jump boot
hits land. Whatcha

gonna do without
or with or do it
to? Unremarkable

shorthairs sizzle off in superheated breeze.
What factor of stability buys off this lack of alibi?

What was that tune you had us singing before things began to move, an ideal in the air around us marking the entailments of a step we hadn't taken yet? As we dogpaddle upstream through steep streets inside a transparent envelope of water rushing down from on high to make even trash and unpatched asphalt objects of religious devotion, we really really want to know. At the gas station parking lot the cascade craps out, or shunts around behind the house on the far corner, a certified historical preservation site assuring us we'll live on through the end. To realign ourselves with the flow of things we'll have to knock and traverse the interior, but we get lost as always once inside and the short hand jumps forward several times between the front door and the attic where we end up. "It's a mother-fucker, but to know it's to forget it," the sudden caretaker instructs us, and we wonder whether it was something we said.

Your mouth would hang paper
over a housing block of moist mix
each fucks off to a private corner
I'm not. Just my sunblind luck

you have to stand
to the back of the head
shoring up the loving crush
of aspiration under pulmonary pressure.
Or the air between our bellies
there was predawn sex you
want this mission, any mission, for

its sweet aftermath
halfway along the walk to work the
sameness of the park and all hope
gone to one of many wars.
The world burns off between the lines
of early light in front page sidebars —

over every wall —

the peopled air settles in an ashy cake
neither waiting room nor fantasy
I'm yours as well

as tall as the tops of your shoes
and think of what you've done to free labor
with a shim to fit the suck of trade to space.

Is a thing shared by all?
Were there the same
shits and grins awaiting us

along the path of greased resistance,
meetings and engagements of a day's forces
for nothing more breathless than breathing room?

And all the action in each seedy interval.

Nothing manages to rise
like a rage for hoe-fired peasant breads
nor yet some third term flickering
as I can be when I recall
the state my lungs are in.
And twice as wide reins in the survey map:
one word negates itself as verb and noun.

Or something fabulous, indifferent to comparison
deep down the vernacular of x-ray, radar, drama.

The inestimable core fries atop the foreign bureau's heat bill,
timed to start before a brighter season kicks up dust

                                        (like an infield fly
        your aesthetics of democracy threw my ballgame
        against the darkened heads-up LCD.
        This overhead perspective in slo-mo rewind
        serves a twelve year half life as remedial geography
        to ride its horse hard from Central Asia west
        into a future in the nineteenth century,
        which after flashing past the piss test
        in the loser's locker room, turns sharply
        to the right of reason. Hit play, dumbass,
        this is what we paid to look at, sitting
        in the dark imagining our soles stuck in crude
        detritus by the merciless flare. That's the filter
        going easy on the eyes, blue toward the meltdown,

        the even break the fielders couldn't find.
        Do people set their fires to fit
        the lack of smoke? People do.

...and the high arc hits close to home —

To the backyard dog
leashed to the perimeter fence
in the academy of part-time counterinsurgents
where citizenship barks against its narrow pass: here's
music that coordinates who's off the grid with
stream on stream of golden light showering
toward the opposite horizon.
You can see it all from here
down to tables of the price flux
that up through the ground come a-bubblin'.
Pulling hair clogs from the swirling water
a self-cleaning mechanism in your mouth
comes around behind to swipe a body clean,

          strained circles of turnover leading from the rear.

                    ✦

          Along the return path
          something more than letters
          less than command unprompted
          by a gesture of mismeasure this
          class is always meeting plants in small talk
          what the ballot bought into jail free but blind
          contour of what inside snitch's self-defensive
          kiss after kiss to smack the cell wall

its membrane stretched across a rising margin
fixed distance over broken ground

                    keep me lyric here across the bridge
                    talking Pacific cargo blues without your tongue
          say hello stranger / put your lovin' hand
          in mine and feel it growing hot it
melts into air like you
just don't

" The third city grows water in its head," they wrote us from there. They wrote us from there to here, our here filling up with their there like how much dirt in a hole of a certain size, an infinite regress tunneling into the suddenly foregrounded gaps in our municipal substance, until the streets themselves grew porous and the waters came up. This far out I can't recall who mentioned them first, but they came up just like numbers in the lottery that picks the ones who must submit to flood. Extreme attachments — the automatism of where one stops for coffee on the way to work, or the side of the street one chooses so as not to have the rising sun in one's eyes — obsolesce by minute intervals of creeping damp. This was the reason we sent the expedition and guaranteed their hourly wage, but now they write us here with injunctions. "Don't," they warn, "ask about the first city, or the second. We had our reasons for leaving."

fresh detail leaks

becomes a date
fate recurs fathering
pre-emption of itself
the wire hidden
behind the arras
memoir's buried depth
faltered into light

forms a tent
retraced retracted step

spans in view
to lick imponderables
what nobody knows
is the trouble
I've seen tongue-tied
bluff a forced hand

                              (into the aquifer –

If that's what you call a nervous meeting over drinks
because the stockpile in the freezer's good for the duration,
then the right to be indefinitely marked bills unfound
where the sun don't shine but all day long
as the day is long and the fabric rich is the click
answering from points where drill hits ore, or
like sand fused into heavy lumps of glass

                          tumbled smooth until it's
                          broken shards of tumbler

               arrayed against all evidence
               called proof, as in 180, it
               is pure grain of that about-face.

Something in the line of march.
Stutter steps right off the table
with gravity to spare and then some
deep wet dream of heavy metal soil

WHERE ALL SIGNS READ NO SPLASHING

What do you call the distance
of a 2000 mile ocean swim
treading water in the unresolved? The weather
holds. The penguins surf their floes
of melting ice against a rim of habitat. One
feels elsewhere an imperative. The rest
follows the foreseeable course of things.
And so the rest follow. The concrete pond is
"not the coast of South America. There's
nowhere to go." And 26,000 trips
to get it right. Fix guesswork on the map.
Small compass of my smaller heart
points

        plotted on a perfect circle
        falling back and back into that
        place along the curve it comes
        to lap itself.

No One Lacks Permission

that you call into
how little we know
is not fate but its feel
and the ocean's cold
thinks for oneself
is recoil in the flesh
where the splinter turns
bits of earth to hand
the moon up its well
and truly almost full
enough to know it's dark
outside the locked phase thin
sliver of new tense that came
Jocelyn to wish your birth
to have become not
compact of the simple
past alone but company
in this as well

Today we assembled to review the architect's model of the new museum, disassembled and spread out flush with the ground soon to be covered by galleries, atria, and interactive visitor kiosks, though the act of covering in this case will end up terminating in its polar opposite as a planning process committed to the full account-ability and transparency of its claim on the future has made neces-sary an exactitude of correspondence between intent and execution to such extent that the realized museum will answer its model in presenting a profile so low as to slip under the threshold of presence altogether. "We have come together," said the project manager to the gathered thousands, "to guarantee that our speaking precisely maps the field of a speech we suffer singly." Reading the accompanying leaflet, we passed over en masse from demand into data.

You lose more slowly —

what's left of a rough night
is what we dream about the dream
next morning Tanya says of ghosts
in marine fog I guess they're ghosts
with guns they want to take us
back an hour or two. Children too,
their wheels and the little wagon
cling in ridges of a fingerprint.
When you think of gravity this way
to overflowing in another episode
which is to say I knew, she says,
faces in the street would be what came
to me at night because the titles
in the dream spelled out part
two of three. That part was the worst.
The very worst. Well, that and you
still whimpering fantastic mammal things.

                    Where the track runs fast
      boils down to headache, loose bowels, debt
      the text of dream, no theory of stages this
      good materialist account in spooky swamp gas
      and I guess in light rain that's us as well.
      Or make us ill. Titration of vanishing magnitude

      in which the underground extractions ride.
      Stick the landing on the bank tower's greasy planes
      between poles of wet lust and arid sprawl
      where cliffhanging tribunals carry water for
      the roots and sturdy branches of the only tree for miles.
      Out of the frame to render and eliminate decision they
      come, a *posse comitatus* convened against *potentia*,
      sentences of *"esse est, esse est"* across the range,

installing constituted order. Baby all the money's gone
to make us small. But this actual earth of value's
smaller still, meaner, faster on the draw.

ALL BETS ARE OFF

(for Christopher Hitchens)

To that larger tune you played a part in when it
swallowed you not quite whole, you work your jaws.
For a fish in the stock pond it's a bold move,
but useless when you're gill-hooked anyway.
Were you surprised how small a barb it took
to force feed you into the assembly of that host?

Still the judge withholds the best in show award.
There's a muddy sump full of fresh contenders,
past masters who'll neither die nor face the music.

Come back behind the camera. Join the others
looking forward at themselves. The live feed stuffs you
speechless. Move your mouth as the host does
voiceovers, still looking for your angle when he's
angling for a bigger catch. From comrade you rise up
to be compatriot, floating to the top. Becoming chum.

✦

— *in deep space, commemorating the brief public career of Jerry Thacker
with a fanfare of global market humanitarianism —*

                              called for a bar of rest
                              in the ear-popping froth
                              but stockroom suicide
                              of course it hurts a pinch

to make you grow roots
of armed humane concern
millions gnaw through seedless
winter shelling cold cash
crops now let's talk straight
face ok about this deathstyle
is it jingles cuing movement
in the African market sphere
round with pharmaceutical
demand to know my name is
carbon life my culture's cooked
down to raw comparatives for
measuring accumulated char

You Can Forget to Breathe

To hear it playing out
all around you is to play it,
is to die for ends without
means the score assumes.
Like once you'd have an income
"settled" on you. A pause of
centuries and the word
makes sense again, with
status indicator flipped.
You snooze against a column
back in standing room. The crowd's
mouths drop bugs into your lungs.
Knowledge bases. Aristotle
held that insects never breathe, that
air's just passing through. Before
the morning paper we agreed.
You must remember. This goes on
when you forget what it forgave.

Between each one and the next there is a third where the
city grows without a thought of water in its head. To keep

this from devolving into infinite regress there's police action,
a dance in the very immobility of administrative boundar-
ies. The public having long since left this theater, the lottery
picked her to be the one to cold call them all, armed only
with last year's metropolitan directory. Her embrace of it
might allow her the compensatory fantasy of the encyclo-
pedist, albeit a fantasy time-sensitive in the extreme and
obsolescing by the minute. An hourly wage guaranteed the
fundamental enjoyment of what she did. With nowhere for
them to go but those numbers or the oblivion between edi-
tions, she'd murder or forget them, every one. The city could
be treated thus as well, a single uniform block.

"heard it all before"
from some other room
audience in speaker cone
process ruminant acoustic look

just from recognizing words
necessity evacuates the mouth
spilled lip on own
bad faith in scrutiny
that props developmental staging
this unconvinced but convicted

in empiricism's click track
reality effects oil flow
post-national meant lube it

to run hot neutral
gears down to war

— *it was said* —

        You came to be here a return address
        whose shape squeezes to the point.
        The waves out there are breaking you

stand here to utter crash
with crisis and correction.
Help wanted in the slobber pool.
And worse that I was dreaming

when I wrote this on the steps
of capital crime. Lyric farce apocalypse
revealed you late in last time's next.
It's one more failed attempt to speak
to you with tenderness in letters
slamming through your roof from three miles up.

Rationalization jolts exchange. Scale
here would weigh the tanker less than tare

for *shock and awe,*

from which delivery platforms turn to hear you drool

from mouth to gut an oozing cleft of scheduled aftermath

from year to year renews cast contracts, sucks out lungs
of offscreen extras seared another time for scale.
"He doesn't just send chills down people's spines. He puts
steel in them." And any other place it can be forced

from smoking ground to gears that grind perpetual motion
from the volatized fuel-air mass of production schedules made from
premises of "Your enemy is not surrounding you.
From this we learn your children killed and kill themselves.
If words have no meaning, then evil's not this." But it falls out,
from syllogism through conditional bombing the conclusion
from the height of short logic's long half life. Still things
oxidize and rot. We can outlast the loud applause, being rust.

You must be breathing —
This minor trickle easily drowned

recapitulates the terror on arrival

as hot wind the wrong way scrubs maps.

Blows into ears even foreseen
will work for punches in the mouth.

Out of unvoiced daze the fricative
the lips are almost locked against
blows back as off-the-air white noise.

The pedagogy gets exact. The TV wants you
answering. Atmosphere completes a turn
to bagging you. Speak forever now and hold it.
Like butterfly effects renew us? Whatever, yeah, ok,

so keep it up until it takes

Reading aloud from the toilet

with unconcealed noise

*

…and rousts the usual handheld from our heads.
For presence we heard presents. Talk at me

sloppy sputter of a cavitated pump.
The flesh when full relief is passed.

Crosstalk fills the house
more than I can manage
to dump me back in every entrance.
Stand there twice and never leave.

                                                    Leave
                                    a little time to crash —

                                    There's a slight echo here

                                    whole balls of twine unroll.

MOVEMENT:
: displaced sideways from the onset of hostilities you'll find the regu-
lator valve

                                    When you expose the central
                                    void it lies flat, disappears.

                                    In a jump on running lines
                                    look for the one whose one
                                    dimension's time enough to lay
                                    everything out in strict sequence.

MOVEMENT:
: a kernel of corn blossoms atop the stove with explosive force
                                    Until you break your arm you get
                                    used to coming at a thing from
                                    both sides. You place bets wherever.

                                    You take the dive like anyone.

MOVEMENT:
: deltas of x caught the drift and grew rich, whose workers ate the
reserves, more or less

: it is culturally unique and it's ground rent

                                    — *and space to burn* –

                                    Could we dial it down a bit?

MOVEMENT:
: you came here jamming shells between your teeth to pick apart
what voiced a person singing "cherry ball" –

        Mechanism: the little man sweeps the board.
        Command from information central:
        invent the reset button. The count
        is two, apparently a surplus.
        A thick subfloor of expansion
        in the realm of speculation scores

        points for both opposable thumbs, from
        Black Sea pipeline to South Street Seaport.
        Outputs grow all over. No one
        eats your lunch. Try another
        number, this connection sucks.

        "Needs oxygen"

      as alternative watch news on mute

    star when finished speaking

      endgame

      propagate and blanket
      played by geological engineer

to explain getting smeared against the ceiling
become imagined sex or zero-sum

        rise to set

          sales to home market
          bite of this
          spit earth —

— *when premature is overdue:*

To write your own captions

signals exit: imagine
me in '77 being
talked out of having

the baby, the lesson
focused on my balls

and what they say my body's for,
where had I listened less intently
I just know I'd show by now –

– You bright pax americana,

norming body counts toward the mean,
I'd gulp and grunt and squeeze
out my fucked-up tiny miracle, a little dim
pore in your sunny crop of skin.

He spoke slowly and with great diffident gestures between each word and the next, acting a dance in the very immobility of the language, as if every border were fluid and could be redrawn to suit his need for a pair of pants that best showed off his shapeless body to his friends who had long since left the theater, leaving with him only the command to eat as much of that functional space as his embrace of it might allow, or as if each line could be rearticulated to cut across those routes that would best undress those same friends into the purity of their own fundamental enjoyment of what they did, accumulating functional black-box buildings full of discontinued apparel with nowhere to go, and thus he did his duty by them for as long as every word could be treated as a block of equal size and no friend would return to see him dancing there and believing in it.

THE SCHEDULE'S DEAD HAND

You need cartoonists for the photograph,
evidence of how your evidence would look.
If they remained your last best hope to picture
secret sources of intelligence the
characters in radio plays would live to talk.

I have learned in all my isolation how
to cultivate my own mute leaks. This

is one atom of a generalized new sense.
We'd have grown the organ for the tortured

legible noise floor of compulsion

in all our single acts of strangled babble
had you put the question to us thus. Scattered,
but good to read by, glints from this tinfoil hat:

> *leaning on the scale*

> — carpenters for the scenery —

> this would be the death of that
> gnostic apprehension of
> secrets unmarked in landscape

> To sculpt a hedge of blown sand
> precision rubs out any face

> ruled out by the obsolete
> mandate. For convenience, each

> is every one at base and

> everyone works it off at new
> devalued rates of overflow.

Or unrolling a ball of twine along the walls of the small apartment, hoping to pack it all in but aware of what subsists and how much road there is to cover after hope. Lying flat to wonder about disappearing under the floor. Exhaling hard at that moment to give one dimension time enough to absorb the body as it speculates on what exceeds the line that goes on unbroken to infinity. Breaking then, coming at the thing from two sides at once in order to slip out of structure and out of order altogether, but finding that even chalky detritus holds a shape and makes a mark around the edge, perhaps the edge of a body. Placing bets on what's best done with and then doing it over. That "the walls do not fall" holds true only so far as it's become the defining problem of an age in which you take the dive smack in between them.

Toward a post-Fordist poetics:

Make exactly nothing

and show the proper
gratitude. The world is
on the move, around.

They tell you it comes back.
Because the tape degrades

you have these dropouts. Each
will have exactly nothing. The many and

here I am one of them by

acquisition on big trash day.
Step off my slagheap, motherfucker:

                : it slows for the speed-up.

                Where the ground is richest
                even if the soil's poor
                deference toward growth metrics —
                what makes of return a back yard

                if not a garden — will admit only

                over time to time-deferred

                speculation in poured slabs or
                a few long-range foundations of

                orders you've projected into
                futures unforeseen, it seems

the digging in drives engines of
siege, not the reverse, no matter how
you beep with crisis rolling back.

He woke slowly and with great difficulty, holes for air but no
machine to cycle the flow, reduced to breathless mouthing of the
name of his dream, something nasty in a can. It was the usual
high-angle shot pinning him to the bed, spread out across the
bottom quarter of the frame, commanding him to eat. He did
enjoy himself so. He did eat. With nowhere to go it made a hole
in his face. He did it, added it, counted it among his treasures
or, as if it were a bead on a lengthening string of like beads,
hurriedly tongued the blood from its reflective surface and did
his duty by it, confirmed in his correctness by a matching gesture
playing out across it as a screen. Sealed thus it would keep, some-
where or other, until he could come to see himself believing in it,

before the turn.
— for Q —

You can be sure the bodies there are
plants, as are the flowers
and regalia standing in for them.
If not a human death, unrecognized

pain and fading tenderness, to what end
should we sail? You have sent word, three
words from there, that other port of speech
become a backhoe covering
men in trenches and all night the hot
spotlight celebrates the day of living
flesh turned concrete mass and chiseled name.
"Honor" and "glory" are the brightness of
that constant watch the dead keep doing
violence to life. But "respect": yes, if you mean
to look again. None of us has seen. Shade's what
I wish for you alone with every
other human name in good obscurity.

The walls of the
small apartment were nearly always damp, weeping condensation
in figures others might have taken for a revelation. What she saw
there was not the question, though, as that humid gravity urged her
eyes to lose themselves, refuse to hold their shape as sensation of the
limit disappeared under the floor. He returned often to her in that
moment where he thought to exceed the line of sight that went on
unbroken between them, having been through that together. A minor
tone of complaint had crept into their lovers' small talk in that place
and, drying, left a chalky ring to mark its edges. Best not to be done
with it. Worse to hold it true.

Worst of all to buy it —

"America goes shopping from the bottom."

Two things at the beginning:
marks by which they're recognized.

And also duct tape. They meet

each other in this art of love.
Fables sell secret partnership
where the nexus disembarks, and
the view through plastic traps heat as
friction in the linkage bumps and grinds.
Dimwits of effective demand!
Secure thyselves with currency
a private booth, and freak me hard
as striptease in the safe room,
answering what's not the question,
cautions us to heightened states of
business burning into orange,

"up to about here":

An urgent need to have them
and an inability to control them:
encoded deliverables en route to

making beautiful music
of the synthesizer pre-sets.

As a prototype or total symptom
still rebukes foot traffic for as
long as tires melt, ride the rims
till wheels come off at fixers' line

items a.k.a the infrastructure.
Enough, my bones are busting out.
Like what passes through the x-ray goggles
undress isn't useless. It only works
too hard equating seeing through
with nothing there to see.

(Pointing to the lips):

— for Tanya —

facing pages of deleted
recognition scenes but faces
press together nonetheless
out of circling footprints or great

needling pangs the weathered sky shoots
inside a body not yet ours
what will be arms unarmed so is
now to a place like a low bed
bounding space for odd limbs even

the superfluous fourth hand trapped
between our navels but alright
I like that softness on both sides
even the knuckle hair loves you
unheld to hand to come with you
out of war and empire fumble
this book and hold a flower up

as if prepared to speak —

References to today's events
have been effectively omitted.
A cage match isn't always
loose figures scribed in squares.

"Down through the mid-50's
we broke loose and had the street.
Batons, horses. There were women
holding children and the cops just…":
this too breaks loose before we cut
back to NASCAR. Think I'll use
the phone, call New York. Maybe Alan will
be home, or Laura, one voice or two
to make it loud as I presume it was,
enough to sing above these engines.
To where however many millions draw
a new geometry, hold on, I'm coming
to it — the point, larger than the circle.

For Oneself in the Mass

— for Devon —

Must include the most important here

at the start, so as not to forget:
"What matters is speech, not speeches."

We walked. We did not march.

In black or in bright colors
eliding the end of this sentence is
the knot to wrap the gift I'd give you.
Examples: the man like our father would
explain how peace whose foundation
is raw matter of war is
no peace at all. The man like you who came

to play drums, give rhythm to struggle,
go through the rudiments for you,
this day we count ourselves many as two.

Every evening on the train home the voice on the intercom barked a ceaseless stream of numbers into the crowded air around her head because it loved her in her frozen mobility across the yellowing landscape that bulged and rippled in the buckling quarter-inch plex of the window, into whose surface some hand had gouged the coded message, "I will teach ANYONE the secret all great singers know," perhaps with the sharp teeth of a house key. Her skin, each time she pieced this sentence together against the flickering background of houses and shipping docks, would feel taut and shiny, as if the secret of song itself were germinating already in her blood. One night she tried humming the touch tone melody of the appended phone number and, finding it perfectly charming, went home to pack and moved that night to a new town full of buses but without a single train.

...and its dispersion into fixed investment

displaced sideways from the outset

kernel blossom real-time in fecal plume

impasto delta drift caught
no-option drive enchain to relay

be face to face of air
natal terrain rule anew
not by ground rent solo
through rent ground came up same

cherrypicked pickapart shelling
grained vox broadcast populi

deliberate as a visible hand:
come to the crux of it. "Democracy

is a beautiful thing." We get hung
in the gallery, value added to the chamber
floor. Conversely, tax givebacks should read
in horizons wider than simple patronage,
being the "setting free" of money capital

to be drafted into military
"reconstruction" programs
in an occupied Iraq, unemployed
accumulation siphoned off

to speculate in the immovables.
So much forced to hover free and clear.
If assholes flew we'd have an airport here.

"Hold that remote,"

    crossing line to make space

    as trial balloons englobe

    $s + v$ sphere of static

what rangefound target wrapped
far face of surface curve
seen and raised relief

    pressgangs atmosphere
    of unreplaced equivalent
    into state wards
    as words' coincident force

      is to buy a dance off shaken ground
    is the pornographic sky starred
      gaze a millionth heat-dead variant

to command the air

legitimate itself there for taking

pressure squeezes out their use
boost fader to max gain

around the psychic Mercator
trajectory converging downsize
decompressed lung to child labored breath

shocked loud vacuum
into which gap
bonds issue
                will guarantee the pre-amp only

by means of watered drink or water
drunk with runoff somewhere and hide
tanning in the undisguised solarity

...*so as to skew the survey*

Called "unimproved," the land
got us before we got ours.
To move the line enclose

in barricaded olive groves.

The fisheye bulge of state vantage,
advantage to the private sector crutch,
props the woodsy commons

all the way to pulp.
People who hit
people are
the luck

of the draw. That stacked deck's

what extends the grift by other
means the option exercised:

>   *the buried trigger*
>
>   rose up flush to meet its ground
>
>   The plane where it maps the field

            flowers in the peephole
            of the people who bear suffering singly
            arranged before them in bouquets

        Your nose all over
        the hidden fist behind a gift
        gives odds you'd stand to read the leaflet

        freeing you up into the foreground's
        handshake protocol with a howdy target
        call yourself acquired.

                              You've been there before:
that other room without windows or even sightlines, with its sound
of muttering and cursing where a social mass is held in wait as an
audience for its own fumblings toward a public speech full of half-re-
tracted insults and the things one claims to have said on buses. You've
recognized a word or two in that speech to make necessity of your
habit of evacuation, your lower lip spilling wet remains of articula-
tion on the chin you stick out in the face of your own bad faith in
other people's spontaneous self-organization. These props develop a
hemispheric stage for your conviction in their priority. Their empiri-
cal reality clicks in the rhythm of your walk, of the fluttering needle
on a nation's oil pressure gauge. It proclaims you neutral —

— draws the unseen volute body

whose thorn still buried in the flesh

    falls to heavy pieces
    of song
    in song.
            Scoping out the romance
    one says they mass for the foregone
    in an art of non-appearance
                whose talent for the obvious

itched and ran.
Hit skin with a suit
unclear in the nuclear muddle

    artful bramble and garland once
    stirred to anesthesia. Flake on unfelt
    in deepening tactical shade,

away from the conclusion.
(anniversary poem)

Might take nine years, say, to work its way

out of the exhaustion of its form.
There could be a treatise. Better to sing.
Best that words don't count for all that much,

until they write themselves upside down
at the back of a loved eye. Beloved, I mean,
they right themselves. Slumping out of shape
has a counter-gravity in that look

and is the privileged laugh
in which we clothe each other's nakedness
the better to uncover it. All our things

settle, nothing is settled, talk orbits
as the undiminished distance between
our bodies, and really, thank god or inertia for that.

Imaginative reconstructions

back up from the abandoned sub-basement…

       *

    …but what they qualify of airborne junk

      sans mirror and decoder ring
      how high the crypt
      just breathe advised empire
      of uninvited archaeology

what sounds dimensions of the annexed valley
anticipating unsealed ruin wherein
are plans for armatures boosted out of burning

      though the words may be wrong and
      the haze is always higher up

STAND IN FOR THE SURVEILLANCE TAPE

until the neck knots forever and a day

more becomes a line, two more a constellation

is impacted order not to be untied

         where supply chains cut
         measure in the wills of the dying
         those burnt remains precipitate
         a mass of undiscovered continents

hectoring militarist evangelism
even bourgeois political economy
without sense of dividend to come

quicklimed faces on the train no more
than resistance in materials, how this morning builds…

…until the automation comes online

Some injured illusion of one more chance
says water's on the rise. It will
become the next big thing. Condense

except in case of vapors, foul miasmas.

Who drained the marsh into the cooling tanks
your fainting spells collect? Fan yourself and sniff
ammonia. "In the exhalations of Americans
there is a crumbling empire." The empire

is always crumbling, on the verge of tears. This
is what makes of it an empire. You look like
you could use a break. Lie down right here.

Space between the rise and fall in series. Waves pushed up
onto a beach. Your sigh returning from abroad as wind.

The weight of one specific body left behind a dimple in the pile of the thick shag carpet. They counted themselves each morning up to greater or lesser degrees of mute facticity but everything came up the same, balanced on the pivot of a missing "one." "We are all present, and present all the way," they wailed, "and yet we do not cover every surface of this life except by adding to each white plane of a blank page a laundry list of limp and murky complaint. Our unspoken imaginings are oddly more specific than the beds we make for ourselves, head to toe here across the length of the room. Blankets drape us as a single body or mass noun waiting for the clothes to dry. The line breaks, though we sleep well." They put on weight together and for each other's benefit, never singly, never knowing what to do with it.

TAP THE KEYS TO NO AVAIL

Knocking holes in a "simple, conjunct melody,"
stand for either liberation or the dump.
White dots to form a cloud. How many gulls.

                                                                    *

On whose sides beads
the cool air saving up
reserves are marshaled
and the glass drained off

is what was meant.
It was said: "The point
in cataclysm of catastrophe

what we thought abstract." Glass
bloodies your foot en route to stain,

while the processor locks —

— the cadence is the first to go

no concords kiss the puckered scar

ornament a habit
banked social spew
forces in desert waste
        to backward view of dark flesh

is focus or confession
the snapshot unbundling death to retail

 demands immediate realization
 fingered purchase cutting sand

You Parse Commands a Line at a Time

As you break step to approach the bridge,
please note the regimented rhythm beating

deep inside the non-periodic,
where muscle knows itself as spasm.

Wrapped up in newsprint and cardboard
against the cold glass brick, all generators
pump heat to the interior until
the building burns. Warm your hands

is advice come crashing down from above
to reconcile firestorm with windfall.
As an image: bat-bombs. Random animal spread

to balance the equation "people = territory = state."
You zero out collateral damage when damage is
the world collateral for world money debt.

 Starting with the headline:

 The buzz from downstairs follows,
 inside the alto's otherwise sweet sound

 a rasped touch of alarm that cuts
 "Take Five" across the grain,

to read yesterday's news
not departing from today's
time. 8:30, same as always
at the second fading chorus.

What this guy plays, its substance

is precision, he's like atomic
clocks for station platforms.
But there's that edge that
hits you like a paper cut inside
the mask of his best Desmond.

The redraw sequence jumps:
after a short i.d. break
click of a chambered round
i from me on waking
or drowning in the wake

with an eye to storm
fronts drop back deep
in the pocket idol's head

lives there to reject

number and mass of the offer

gives pleasure shaking no
against intubed flesh take off
your clothes and say procedure...

...over the unminded gap
— for Thomas Carney —

You can, if you want, see shapes
in the text of your world record

pasted to the window
they come straight through

to get to you. Dry wind does
bring back something wet,
a spray of color onto paper

saturated to translucence.
What simply gets along with want

simply drops out through the pane
and yes, we're bodies pressed close
against the glass, mutual anger
in that irritation, those layers.
And how would this differ from love?

"A burst of static":
in the air around buildings
an ideal to approximate.

Or the transparent envelope is
the balloon frame in itself in which

see yourself inside the seeing-through
to studs. Plat or plumb-bob self-posits
to posit self a start before
the start to live on through the end.

There is fire, not as frequent

as before, but unavoidable
from time to time the gas main
blows the short hand forward. To know is
to forget it, digging up shards
along the seams that craze the landscape,

turning air inside out

dense cloud of birds

    or isn't it the turbine's job
        the desperate body heat expands

    where "we can only stay tuned or stunned"
    as the blueprint of a jagged hole
nonetheless rips the sky with electronic screams

though a "periodically necessary structural adjustment"

    as in camera the negative horizon
    sucking up a vacuole
    to process flesh into down and paste
        to glue the flock together

            as prelude to the dream-work:

            Dissolve to a crowd
            waving hands.

            To come in after the finale
            in the hourly-rate motel, breathless

            in the dark, waiting to scream.
            "Surprise!" Knock, knock. Cop,

shines flashlight in. More waiting.
2 a.m. Knock. At least they bother,

but still no birthday, no citation.

Slip across the highway
bordered in azaleas, make tracks
into quaint antique theme village
under cover of the sudden
daylight. Swim the flooded street:

"The things one says on buses and
in lines are character studies for bad songs one should forego the ef-
fort of writing. Other people's spontaneous self-organization sets the
warm, smelly air to humming a melody more beautiful than anything
one could call art. Against the priority decisions of hemispheric trade
or the bitter complaint at the driver's heavy brake foot that passes in
hocket from mouth to mouth down the center aisle, one can arrange
no more elaborate orchestration. One's veins and muscles are always
fluttering as if jabbed with oily, painless needles by each person walk-
ing past on the way to the exit door, and one grows first accustomed
and then wholly dependent on that anesthetic shock. In the end one
remembers only old songs for which one had professed blank disin-
terest, and asks in reflex, 'When will I be loved?'"

It is frankly disjointed.

Mass producing signs
in solidarity. *We stand*

united against us.
Reporters at the front

"embedded," *lit and
shot in high duality.*

Traffic dodges man
Market and Kearny who
chides his duck
in quiet Mandarin, gently
stuffed headfirst into
paper bag. From this
scenario the heart
is lacking for connection.

                    And this is its measure:

                    of time as mass
                    as if a brick as

                    if a bomb a
                    clutch of plastic toys

              motion capture role of
              public intellectual working quality control

                    in dildo factory is

              mass sufficient in the mass
              individually as in mass
              producing wall clocks' congelations from
              this condensery locative ambivalence
        built in time rushes out
     counting down prone through
blast blazed away doubling back —

                    Made evident by cutting
                    the same might be said, one
                    unit of the general collapse.

                    Bus turns back halfway.
                    In plastic bag forgotten

breakfast swings against thigh
on the way to the underground,

the thought, it must have started then.

The single bodies, their dance
of the near-miss, the nod,
the randomness consoles.
To be otherwise convinced
of pattern: this is
nothing large enough. Heads
of the town sound off.

THE STATISTICIAN'S FLESH

Stand up and be undercounted!

    +

More than you will ever know

to plant oil stains on the denim
we're all in all together.

    +

Is a duet.
The double unseen

is not secret. Is
secreted. Neither fragment
nor hologram, but sticky mass

                stretched between attack and decay

                says void space around the slogan

드drugged with what

none yet can want

one star sufficient

for the astrologer his
day of truth also
drops dead a sun

must not rise at 6:18 a.m.

The sound of speech names the speaker's death.

"What good's a groundwire
without ground? The arc burns out
the circuit as the current

takes on visibility." Thus the text

hopes for a text
of hope. The war

for unlimited expansion
of fate will not be

fate itself. "This just can't
happen," giving way to, "This
can't just happen," marks
the burn pattern that recalls

where the heat input originated.

An Infernal Syllogism

If flow means invariably
downslope and speech
means time as money
equals shit whose hill
grows higher while cities
sink in flux variants
the drain can't afford
means to choke down a mouth
for words equal to the breath
of fecal aspiration
in the amnion, and if the first
fluid wealth must always
ooze out the ass-end of
time, then hills arise
before the city is and
this is birth and so this is
a poem about the death
of George W. Bush.

And without conclusion,

what it says and nothing more
slips in its "peaceful entry
of force" simply to display what
still rolls its presses of a will to
deceive and be itself deceived.
In the middle of the poem
Joyce's compliment: "Not even
at work and already writing notes.
So organized." Not a word
I'd have chosen. Reduced scope
of any single act today.
Scribble on the sidewalk in chalk
what the military server bounced:
"For you, dear Quinton, peace. And
peace to whom you'd kill, peace
to those who aim at you." But to you
who make the rolling unsay all:
may you never rest again.

DATED JUST IN TIME

We dream about the dream next morning in misguided conferences, hoping that our assignation might lead to the assignment of collective guilt that absolves us of the weight of one specific body left behind by a heavy sleep as a stack of discarded drafts or minutes that no one at the table will ever read, but which must be filed and preserved nonetheless. As children, too, we did this, and with a greater degree of easy bad faith. The ridges of a fingerprint showed through every surface of a life admitted in advance as forensic with the loss of the auxiliary verb between, "You made me do it," and, "You made me." The latter was oddly more specific than the former, being part two of three die-cut plastics specified by the model kit for building a fort. Draping blankets over bunks was the worst. And the very worst of us slept well there, that's how. Next on our agenda is what, and what to do about it.

We Might Not Occupy but Live

— for Wendy Kramer —

The street is now substantial
to our being. It leads nowhere
but where we stand, arms linked.
Close in behind the passing phalanx.

Tell the woman next to you,
"This intersection is now yours."

While you share the water she offers,
not distinguishing this nourishment from tears

blurring the view ahead, recall
that the missile saw quite clearly
the wall it had to breach in looking
for a child, her legs athwart the new map.
For whom will we shore up this space
that cuts between us, if not for her?

AND READY FOR THE STARS

Beneath nothing but sky

     as the anchoring invention of zero
     but downscale in explosive tons

     we'll arrive at ten

       chained in pairs
or rainfall from inside us

     spotted by the optic nerve
life in weeping pores
     for shelter from the shade

       where light fails to reflect what
there we'll build

You sometimes fail to look up,
remembering where it came from:
a Third World it had made, never had
the sheer beginner's luck
simply to find. We're tired.

Drooped over stations on that line

        hand to hand
        handing water

        up the grade
        of hand to mouth
        to well within

the blast radius is us, falls
on us too lightly. Even desert flowers
pollinating air would weight us more.

Where the stroke falls:

function of the closing chapter on
colonies. How hanging out
in parking lots prepared it

        to prepare you

        to receive it
        in your body

        is that discipline
        clenched in common
        air you wait to breathe

outside the ventilator. Breaking bottles
on the pointillist marimba punctuate
sustained belief in the event.

     The contract takes hold.

     Aftermath is to begin
     invokes a row of lampposts
     for new owners of the grid
     lock in those contracts

     with a test run in Bolivia

          simply cup hand
          another fist produces

          manageable units
shiver
timbered sky fallen

mass into sharp-edged ziggurat
not popular populated base of bleeders
water the roots of mess

because there is as yet no manifesto against blinking —

In miserable times, one shows up
in time to take these notes
no one will read. In these
United States I am a poet,

          embedded. Today Bill Marsh suggests
          we work to process information.

Where information circulates as
      psy-ops through the total value product,
        a whole lot hangs on the character
        of that process. Never have we lived
with more data, nor with less demand.
We declare ourselves for taking hold
and smashing tables that describe a world that works
      only if the 500 golden birds
        return to department I,
        which first sent them flying.

      This reflex freezes in the frame.
      Simply for the pleasure of standing in line
      one seeks out administration.
      There is enjoyment in the brush
      of hairy arm on arm
      on the bus. The DMV draws up

          analogies for streets already dim
          in hindsight of twenty or a hundred
             simply standing
             in each other's void

      of fading presence. What
      deeper diminishing cuts we will
      accept. People die miserably
      for want not *of*, but *in* what
      is found here. Care to take it outside?

        ✦

      With a title at the bottom
      the letter writers come.

      And in the tangled hair
      everyone must dream

to its full, terrible height. Bite
with our tiny rat teeth.

Meaning none
too bright, overexposed.
Backlit chihuahua
dwarfs colossus who

walks him in my
experience of sticking
to routine. Things
you see come up
alongside funerals.

✦

...we can dispense with the dispatch

and the language comes to this

blood and bits of leaves
vividly then arise

impression of cracked teeth

have anything to say

menaced shadow of itself
talks and talks demob

backyard's unexploded
fragments into nose
and ears the better ordnance
to hear you burrow in

skipping back to aftermath.

A synchronic history of pacification:

as the British cut off
water the U.S.

cuts the phones.

Then say it:

standing too close is
enough to be counted for

the same in either calculation
of "what could not be
calculated in advance."
All the same, the same dead time
advances. Nothing adds up.

Everybody gets a digging stick

to be, and not

stageist "theories"
would pack it all in
as cereal settles

"where'd I get this boil?"

sun you're glad of

too goddamn bright
wrong eyes ahead

through night scope
green, but *theirs are red*

tick off civilians
down to zero

— though this is "not a human right":

appear, or come unclothed.

Without place for villagers' self-defense
except where it pokes through skin
grain of air-time's constant.

Well, what did you rub up against?

Providential wind you're not

or not nearly dumb enough.
You see by lack of focus

almost the periphery of vision
and set rods against cones

by posing them in uniform
degrees of the republic.

       ✦

"The chick was in the way"

       ✦

Liberation narrows to force
an opening of arms in
whose absence open fire.

⋆

And so it's time

to stop. No more
petitioning to be

heard. Inscrutable
in local dress is how
resistance mounts.

the head voice cracks

mute issue of the point

but *polis is eyes,* saw you in
the warm street bare limbs
exposed to all that violence ill concealed

second point a line

looks like it's

the bombing of
a city, but it isn't

earth that gives way beneath apartments
this groundlessness piles up

bodies for the rough topography
of a forecast map

The salt extraction lake is a barrel at monstrous scale, or else the salt itself is sugar and the plaque that cakes your teeth here commemorates impurities accruing to you through smiling contact with a global trade regime. So someone thinks, walking backward on the berm. The factory floats atop her sightline on piles sunk into its crust. This shelf of earth I pace, she mutters, is a balcony at the prince's summer villa, and will collapse. When the film is processed you will see how the quaking in her legs determined the composition of the shot. There was a missing step but such nostalgia has a strictly emetic function from the limited standpoint of the photographic frame, which is beside the point. She thinks now of the block, whether child or tumor, that the next necessary breath will pry from her. The coming step, too, will crumple the nondisclosure document underfoot. A checklist of names will remain in place of that nothing. Fluid noise from the tide pumps.

BETWEEN REGISTERS

Is segmentation

the head's duress
as the hand scrabbles
for a name in public fact?

Saying "purple tree" is

its failure to have known

what it clenches out.
"Little dog." "Late model compact."

And the haze thrown up
around a park or square.

Moving in divisions. Famous
noms de guerre remain.

         The image blurs

         indigestible part of the line

         you're fed
         in place of who will starve

         the siege

         victory declares

         itself to have been always

and always on the way
as Rome resorts to vandalism

             ...this is to say a twining of the coarse
hairs that line the posterior surface of the free limb around the
barbed projections on the wall that sets a limit to the consequence
of climbing. A model or a doll, to demonstrate this in detail, would
be a marvel of contemporary design. The mouth closes in around
the tongue just a bit too tightly. Into that anarchy we found yester-
day while straining to draw its exact proportions from sequentially
layered sheets of onionskin, hungers had been artfully dropped from
a great splattering height. Stroke his leg no more than three inches
above the upper edge of the patella, along an imagined diagonal run-
ning from the small toe to the scrotal terminus of the perineal seam,
then grasp his left nipple and twist ten degrees clockwise, as illus-
trated in common practice chord theory. A thick paste of conclusion
is internal to his sensibility. Here you articulate the thing it burns

              in a rack focus

              made of twine or hair

              and it passes through
              the doll who doesn't eat

              mouth a pre-fab o
              closes in on somewhere

              a draw strains account

              of the theory of phlogiston

              internal consistency
              a thick immovable paste

              toward being burned by air
              with its articulated limb

◆

– A tongue of background slips forward.

The substance of a Roman debt
                              is
                    the debtor's body,
                    portions

            into which it can be cut
            represent the sums

                of money

of its several claimants.
                              Thus Linguet.
            Or Rumsfeld, off book: "The oilfields
                    of Iraq
                          are
                    the Iraqi people." Subject and object
find premature false unity in this
Caesarean birth of late Enlightenment.

◆

OUT OF THE CONTAINER
            – for the Oakland demonstrators and dockworkers of April 7th –

As balance of payments,
also balance of force
as counterweight. Even beat cops
muster out for the domestic army.

The ocean current it slips along
under steam, the timing

of returns, the circle, revolution
in the means of transit. Turnover

cuts time down to spin.
Buy the strobe-effect and everything
looks comfortably solid. Then you're
caught in turning blades, or
face the rifling grooves. All power to
the body moving
slowly, when it moves.

                    And into the hole —

            toppled statues' unstable equilibrium
            states for any possible witness
            can't be poem but omen today

                        had it dead to
                        rights the rank and file

                        draped flag over face
                        fact of claim staked

            down to property till brass
            doxology renewed its lease on
            lifelong leashed reports' front
            constabulary mission to back
            prospects for a holding company
            standing on the selfsame plinth

sinking into futures
curve inflects an accent
on name for the equation
holds the line from who to how

come camp exxon pitched like
x-ray over broad fields
of localized euphoria less local

anesthesia for triage amputations
literally uncounted figures that

"we just don't know we might
as well make up a number" which
motto serves as well the graft
of perle brigades cast before
their own advance along the long
deferred march of freedom to flow
of sweet light down the pipe's wide bore

    with an ear to distribution
    storm the calm with freon tube
    hubcap mixed bag of document
    and ornamental fixture set to strings

    the voice goes under in murmur mix
    to surface in deluxe anniversary
    editions ten years hence

    faced back in warning
    what you think is happening is

    even and especially off
    camera obvious and simply not
    enough relief to go around
    the corner and take cash
    value discount on a bag of
    viscous water half an aspirin
    to no music wait the new collapse

or hear not music but the orchestrations,
out of which a voice: "I want
to exercise my right to free speech
for the first time in my life. Please get

out of my country."
In any case — which is
the difficulty he's in, with

us, that whatever advocate is
in the drama regardless, as in

not looking at it, reading off
coordinates — horizons hide
behind smoke. Rather, smoke rises
to cover, in evidence of
battle that is fact of matter
productively consumed. All that so far
in your face the eyes roll back

             crowding out the room noise
             some things good to know
                  that there are some
                      things unabsorbed or not

                absorbed for good but stay
                to grow their barnacles
                this bottle from last century

                  clinking on machine parts
             Slips for those who wouldn't leave now

                stacked dry by the bombed container
              What we come to as a city
             from ground turns to
                  land here and sinking deep
                    in mud shod in salvage
                      copper and lead the metal
shop on standby for new lightshows

WITH ALTERNATE ENDS

You — or at least to see you —
and here are others
mopped off the counter for unrolling.

Until the milk turns
required salt and oxygen,
still intoxicating as pointless

exercise the right
to not. Something something

triumph arching back
accentuates rump elements
blah blah people's militia blah
shot blah themselves etc.
for own goal through
hole in others' heads et al.
To be done, and not be well

you have to stagger start times.

In that sense to keep the hand out
rendered docile and this is

the form of organizing
on the parceled ground.
For the water-hoard air trades
as it is long-winded on the run

to oscillate and hold those
contradictions firm in public mind

with lack of resolution.
By means of blur
the industry not craft

back of images comes clear
in its particulate dodge and burn.

They lack intrinsic rhythm, unless it is that by which the teeth select and strike them, a face rising from their mass like a cake baking. Someone thinks of walking and as if by grace the ground is there and is not difficult and is the problem. Sight piles a crust on what it touches, the eyes first of all. Those earthenware vessels on the shelf go to sufficient lengths in their coiling to pace off the distance between handicraft's roadside aluminum shed and the specialty shop in which they met another fate. Legs, though, only continue to make sense in being shot out from under the cellular composition of the whole. Nostalgia has room to stand just to one side of every single pixel in the world's largest rear-projection screen. A child's breath, fogging the glass, is enough to thumb the finish off and reveal these thousands of pinpoint tumors on the scan. The foot as measure lies crumpled under the foot that measures these and only these. In place of them, nothing but. Tides pump the shore away to shore it up

but not fall down.

Today we offset funny money
on a twenty-minute indoor cycle.

Kids downstairs out of rain

quietly quietly
rebuild the buildup

arms at speed
in which rotation someone
ends up hit. Five starters

among them
not a single lefty.

The flash of light
that someone overpaid for this.

Below the slab

with a new general equivalent

play at making piles, puddles

of steady liquid pressure
for the midterm.

Say you are become the cyclone.
Tests to gauge kinetic frenzy still
come down beat back to haul up.

Gravity acts at bottom of the cast list

as all that weight resettles.

On the shoulder it's a
dicey proposition if you take what dangles from a view of all your
been-there-done-that's for risk potential in the coming business cycle,
or a fond eye-burning glance over your right flank into sunsets you
steer drunkenly away from, like Hitchens retrenching in a bleary Fa-
bian fantasia of social-democratic empire. When it gets dark outside,
the gaps in that tableau register as a few hummed bars of "Missis-
sippi Goddamn," placed here in honor of Nina Simone, who will die
tomorrow still answering affirmatively to the contrary. Speaking only
for myself, I admit to a blank stare at seeing it cross the border into
praxis on the two occasions when someone bothered to ask the uni-
versal question: "What are you?" It's a difference between two kinds
of ash. Plant the work in a whole cut field.

THE GROUND STAYS WET

(for Tanya's birthday)

a long time to short order

    called collected burst of size through printed circuit

        moment paper floats and rocks

        crop up among returns to hold

   and scrape it both
     are worth and equal

        of any thirty-three years more at
       least one smudged hand
   damp atop another

Longer than weather

and a few quick sparks at the plug

it is the colorless air paints us

irremissible inkling of capillary action

to spread thin signs of wind
high enough to be unseen

faces called self-rule
always of the trump suit

the one screw loose
to hold the wall
the bulb blows out

                 ✦

Shorter Than a Thirty Second Spot

Call this happenstance transcendence
of the haptic splice. It keeps it

dark outside and in

there is a cute conceit
of digits, that open
borders over all
they grasp could be
the brand-new universal.

Ash-flake of scripture,
meet injection mold. The nod
might cop to feeling this that what

gets cut
is not the vision but
the worker in its field.

            ✦

You're a big boy now,
unabsorbed by the medium.
In deferral, phantom limb shared

among the institute of angry idiots

the better to hand out beatdowns.
By that mark shall you know
and then forget. And eat bananas
for your breakfast, bruised fruit

of a really bad idea
soaking up last night's atmosphere
with surplus attitude and blatant
boycott labels. Punk as fuck

shakes moneymakers not
to stir. Sucked sweet nothing
wanting nothing in the straw.

With new alternate ends
swimming in the large
leaves a glut of stumps

to begrudge the one-eyed
blank face cards.

This is the same product
carried by our boys.
I swear it turns to mush in there,

what else can I say?
Today I left the air out of tired
resignation. Late report
up the org chart, I jiggle these here

fleshy globes. Self-action
drains an ear into my vacuum pump.

For Radical Librarians

A particular hand breaks the surface
in a shower of bright drops. Blood, or

rose water, from a chemical pump.
The archive is occulted with the imam.

Agents and reagents here have broken

bread and ground up into oil of account,
byproducts off the books: bodies, dust, paper.

American kids blow hard on chemistry sets and
hope experimental smoke will clear. Four thousand
years, displaced, held suspended between borders,
to precipitate when the reaction cools.
Land records, too, diffuse throughout a global
circulation. They are a claim on every ground.
This will come as revelation, not surprise.

With an Ocean to Make Weather

(for TB and JK)

This posture — "straddle the hill,"
what Tisa says, bring your center
down to meet it coming up —

not use we make of the body but

bodies that use makes of us.
John's thinking of topology

to explain why we don't roll back

down to where the talk settles,
a lactic afterburn of words
collecting in the thighs next day.

Tone tracks back to sunlight embouchure,
smell of bottlebrush and salt, wide stances
cut the incline where still we lean to speak.

        ◆

Meanwhile Air Force One surveys facts on the ground

                to circumflex the legs
                to regional pronunciations' edge
                double down or double over and emit

                minor ecstasy of a person of interest
                strangles on the syllabary

                as what spikes a populist vowel
                long ball far
                above the daily rate adjustment

    speaks for these raggedy-ass trees
    that chemical anxiety tongues toxic

    flyover oxygen must be high
    to think to belly-bump
    the general margin's fuselage

for a scaleable theory of land use
around the property the theory
of canebrake counterpunching timecard
process of democracy analysis

terminable and interminable
sense of let's roll broadcast
to the NAFTA diesel fleet
paces off the courthouse green set free
from servitude on jury nullified from
on high strange fruit no tree'd stoop to conquer

in permanent reaction lumbar pain named
RSI of choice for iterative dear johns

i'm only dancing thus al-Zubaidi
struggled with the Karl Rove soft coup routine
another day another thirteen students
laying ground for one more charter school

    ✦

A New Molded Armrest

Tired of being funny, angry, but the weather here
is something else. I can soak up miles
and miles of razor burn,

more every day. *I*
see the sun. I know the sun
is important. I write about it.

For seven hours ask about
lost wax, then look under your nails.
But remember to bend your knee

when proposing to the screen's clean pink face
that it be lifted off the ground. You want a thing

or two, to cover up the round head
ballooning through your hair. Alright,
that one's me, I wing it. I can hear you now.
Small words, solar wrinkles in the radio.

◆

GIVEN THE CHAIR

If you notice any problems (and
you have), please do not
notify the worker. And she has

beeped us out of meeting.
Is what shines on you crazy
dyning in the pitch-field of
chopper blades? They cut

into the flow as it comes correct

off the line, getting stuffed
inside a skin. Apparatus upgrade

named for what the beta version pulped,
a hard look at the Housing Authority calls it
Radical Reconstruction. It's the stock
pile your downtime perches on.

> *I rock to that organic composition.*
> *The rising matter threshold is one.*
> *Apologize for what I penciled out,*
> *rubbed in. Is that two yet?*

Thus ushered in the new age
with infinitely sedimented bands of
oily gray between chucked integers.
To the nub, hello, this has a crack.

I am this big trash. Who stole my pan flute?

Into the case with you, you ticker.
Let me whet my saw. Clip the notice.

Damp walls humor me so sick
today with brain pain. This is
                    the best I do,

dreaming of a private language.
When the stack of plank and puppet slides,
you get to start again. It's pious,
this beaded choke of shut up vast.

Organ pans left to right and
back. And that stands
in for the hitch and wet warble

of contraltos written in advance,
unspooled from the cassette diaspora.

The heart sucks up water
in between. My lake fish died.

I will have to go
to sea.

        And so we were kept busy kicking back
with the luxuriant fluids. In a room of a certain size within a built
environment we often railed against only to witness the self-action of
our invective become outmoded handicraft, so that the act of railing
became the custom burnished railings along balconies whose com-

mand it was always ours to abdicate, an even glow of phosphorescence was the key to lock in our experience of space against phosphorus burning the horizon. That was a mouthful, and we came up just short of choking on the lettered blocks that bit by bit constructed our births into a palpated and sized-up movement. We do not return there, gulping down the limit of each other in an alley. Or else we do, compressed into a mass that sinks below estate.

At Your Desk, a Highly Leveraged Zero

Every day is ground hog day
in the Cargill pork-processing unit.

An elite team of registration pros
can stretch your penumbra with size, snow cut
with small islands, marsh, ophitic structure
coiled about the flesh-stamps. No sweat, just twitch.

It's written that the knife hand often slips,

close to $50 idle protein all the long way up
to your command of standard stencils

in spilled blood and vermiform manure
over cereal monoculture in the new periphery,
to write in tiny burps and gags. Looks
as if the enemy of coordination looks like
futures, more bright winter glare on ink.

For My Autodidactic Asphyxiation

Starting again Monday my grip

on its economy won't secure so much
as discounts bulking up on blocks of type,
the type that blocks a bloop back to the mound,
setting up the rare 1-2-4 double.

Blank stare at 60 feet of
excluded middle walleyed,

loess chemistry's blown
off exam to one side, coriolis

pattern recognition for the moving spikes in
first-person shooter cartridge sales
to the other. One is always relatively overvalued.
Brent thinks I should write this down
before the windup sells the pitch to write it off.

          I'm probably more like a sand flea.

          Without prehensile toes

          the mathematical sublime
          subtends whatever patch of skin
          your post-whatever-else erosive

          crabbed praxis of the gouged-out
          decorative gesture on
          the body of a spun

          commodity can't scratch.
          Party over here, party over

          there, nowhere the question
          of the party. In beached leisure
          I'm all up in your skin, pus in pleasure,
          salt in waistband. In English that
          might rhyme. Here it's rash, and flares.

In Today's Inversion

Can't hold umbrella, smoke, and read
at once. Most often the book suffers,
left back. Barreling through slick odor
of asphalt mist, solo drivers surf
word back inside blank head. Get crammed

      commands to any space by force
      the atmosphere and mobile mark:
      fate, or some nearby pavement.
      "With a decent wetness," yeah. Anyone might care

   how like the bees to be, a history dropped all over town
   by architects until the late season rain
   proves hostile to one side of a fabular mouth, and can't
   leave the other wholly dry. Geography's day planner
   goes without saying in the anti-climate plaint.
   Without saying this is not to say, and stilted, grown
   tall on oil and water. When it slips it counts.

An impossible mix of cheese and value-added research programs straddled the hill of uncharged nylon membranes with their notions of what women should and shouldn't be. That soil today makes use of a body for dry storage of what happened on the urban hike, laid over its surface and covered by a layer of paper towels. A mystery character was thinking of a state in the union of mineral depletion with "critical Americanism" and its rubber sheets, trying to pretend the planet was shaped like a list returned from anywhere with X's standing in. The nostalgia was built-in for blood, and remains the reason we don't roll back without evaporating the hope of national suicide among the indices of current curriculum development. Your own sauce collects on your thighs without this recursion. Stop opting for the light when things get heavy.

A Little Vigilance

I.
In the overheated forcing house, Political Islamist
plays it close with Militant Revanchist Thatcherite.
PI to Mr. T, you have a lovely daughter.
In the painted paradise of a crusade
above your door, I do not think that she will sing

to hear her voice's echo slap as blowback from
the armored shell that hollowly entreats her

to relent and let herself be rescued.

Says Mr. T, for pity's sake, fool, you're
sweating bullets. These lush chemical vapors
burnish my reserve of gold. A tiny woman
once rode my lap to stroke these chains.
She represented discipline along my topiary coif, hard-edged
as the borders I had drawn way back around today's per diem
for a shamus snooping 'round the shame of my employ.

II.
And a stifled yawn,
with a stock disclaimer: This film
has been edited for television.

Deaths and endings have been reassigned
to me and sheet music I'm in bed with.

Getting used to it, I mean, how many
of these things did Miklos Rozsa score?
And why's there so much skin

bunching up around your eyes?
Looking back, it's clear who was
double-dealing whom, but the light
then wasn't like today.

This trite amnesia plot is for
crowds at the premiere, not the dick
going dark behind his halo.

III.
In the middle of the shutout
the PI heckles. "Your city is a brightness

full of filthy grit. I supply a glut of
both, to broaden my angelic emanation,

glory hazing my heroics on the warning track."
Beefy Yankee henchmen help T. into a flex,

menacing the snooper over means of payment.
T., magnanimous, scowls a bonus: "Everybody knows

what you will surface: the body
in the oil sump, my rotten spawn

posing for the wide net of surveillance.
Cut to the chase, for which the new director's cut
rolls out eternities of unseen footage. No one
makes it to his credit line this time."

IV.
We pause here for commercial
and a question: *Who's the absentee whose*

machines and properties obtrude
to stud the farmed-out field of this
production? If that sedan with all its

Lebensraum and mirror-finished chrome
was really commandeered to be abandoned

(the rumor on the set's the seeming extra

who kept that plotline moving got perked
for higher billing with safe passage
to an undisclosed location, and thus

remains at large), *then what rock-bottom terms*
might slip your own remaindered carcass
into slick settlements behind that wheel?

V.
Returning with this nagging sense of lack
viewers — you, more popularly we — find
what they missed at the beginning still intact
inside a truant present. The denouement is canceled,
pre-empted by hectoring public address whose
grain spikes the smooth plain of unrelated broadcasts

wholly owned by Major League Baseball,
thus unaccountable here. There

was never a good ending for this.
Roles went uncast. The writer got stumped
on snappy acronyms for Man from Bechtel,
Onward to the Endtimes Likudnik Antisemite,
and Voice of Invisible Hand of Invisible Man.
All the heavies ended up behind the camera,
killing time with Hawks. It's not just overtime, we need
new tempos. When the grip strikes the set
you need to be there, passing through the screen.

A Newish Musicology
— contribution to a critique of the Weird New America —

your head voice borne under
by the bad wave as in sine
noised up with sawtooth and
three squares to nourish
with comparative authenticisms

digitalis for the digital
bluescreen the blues
when inflection stormed historical

stages counted for a coup
of dice overturning in the alley
where none of this belonged

to you ever this massified address to
the abstract known of systems' metal
shrieking at the foot-pound
overload you stroll along

              ✦

for the best jury possible
washes up around the ears
undulating roll call through
pressure in the room in
the head too squeeze
to temple to temple the forceps

delivered out of separation
into pure fluorescent concept of
separateness empaneled en masse

as polyp coal carbuncle chancroid
growth selected and assessed found
to want — *something* — as only low and wet

horizon the tide strains a larger
number through the shallows most
fucked up on rocks converge
with time on something mean

THE VERY BEST OF CULTURALIST RESISTANCE

Becoming more of what you've heard,
rank and filed-down attentions shoot
the landing in reverse. Reload is cheap
and science is advanced. "Experimental" beats off
by a rational fraction. You can dance, still,

into stillness and the chill.
What I can't believe
is how anyone keeps

writing this, or that
they do. I do it myself, sez me,
cod-utopian option on

idle stock to puff the dollar.
Other guys try to get by. They make it
in buckets, after-market gas. Leveled
field of 'em, frictionless hit at speed.

                    ✦

IMMOLATED WITH ITS WORLDLY AFFECTS

You know you don't get
to control her thumb.
As long as she's not
sticking it in your mouth,
what's the problem?
The game's not going

anywhere, I had
my mission there

ten years back and ain't
tryn'a be *that guy*. Look, Bolivar in bronze!
And fresh beets. No more indigenous
behind-hand cough, please, we're
not scared, just
thinking. Same thing

       in lieu of burial.

       The point, at all,

       or nosing through
       public easements.

       Anywhere from

       this platform check hair
       in window of the big tent

       includes you out trans-interim.
       Your mother but you
       can't bring the marmoset
       on my train, *man*.
       Camped out
       a block from home
       and o, cologne, you
       dense unit plume.

       ✦

GROOMING A SUCCESSOR

of any possible

new comrade pick

today to welcome
chimpanzee to share

in tangled wilds
of this our
genus happy genius

of no house
to teach us

dance and digging
with twig fat
grubs our implements
consume all else

              ◆

— *during a press conference* —

Turn to take it
had to be
this one back

and forth along
the track of the hurricane
fence. Well we have
learned importance

of communication,
won't be shooting

this time.
Line 'em up
is bugged-out code
for citizen review.

For combustion's cast recording:
Between you me and the lamppost

there's maybe half a snowball's chance
to gather speed into the stretch

and roll up larger than life
with an eighth in the tank

and twice as ugly on the crew that works
the corner when the lines are down
or now more often when the center holds

reserves of flow even while the beat of
state capital keeps on bumping distant kicks'
explosive decompression up

against the floor from which one counts
back to hit the one as if it's raining
those don't-hit-me's all over the world,

          remixed with alternate ends.

          There's a finite slice
          of sidewalk, exactitude of
          angles and all

          they might exact from
          each. You think the trashbag knew

          when it was introduced what
          it would introduce itself of
          novelty in set design for

          one and two in mobile
          shelter three the slow
          off-gassing of a dump?

          Up the intervals, what a
          rush. I get off here.

For the overdubbed whistle solo,
raining from cornices not
sky. When it gets wet
here it means you.

Silly speculation on refinement
of the atmosphere under pressure

to distinguish the two cities:
no fun. Anywhere at all
the refinery finds its way to

build a bridge in air
to you. Call that the rainbow

if you like but I won't
dance your plastered little jig.
Even if I'm a rainbow too

or a grace note or two,
— for J.L-H —
a regular form as if
by accident. Round off

excess talk from where your head
wants to learn to turn.
And how to bring your hand to mouth,

taste of rain, taste of milk, of
salt. Dense new hairs like feelers
grab for what's past eyes.

With fractions, intervals of sleep
inflect this numeration into curve,

blow bubbles in a constant stream.

There's a world in there, meeting
chromatic pools on circling skin.

will never abolish
icing fluid noise
kick to sternum

    knocks on phosphor

        bit by bit on blocks
    recon powder each movement
            palpate print bruise to number

            gulps of limit
           moved inside to come
           around from alley

with fierce compressed resistance

                  save by attention

                  It becomes a crystal.
                  To feel across years

                  on a larger scale
                  ache and stiffness in lines

                  that do not break.
                  Into the camp with
                  its own death row

                  an unfigured outward.
                  From the shear and crush
                  of that pressure edges

                  sharpening to slice the writing
                  hand that tumbles its materials
                  smooth will make the cut
                  to last. Analogy, at last.

What's missing in sleep
is not the 60-cycle hum
the demon gazing back

from where one shut it down
or gaping. Mouth breather
that it is it is it is

inside the chop shop
and the boosted writ
small upon own chops

enlarging over work. Not
to say expansive to

say pink slip written
over fair but slack
tongue's title nothing stock
to swipe the not it is to say,

crouched atop your head at dawn,
divided among its four emanations:
breathing fiberglass vapors;
noisy Vaseline marked read me;

art-critical halitosis sermon; and
nonetheless. I religiously insist

being impolite
that they are trebled.
Twelve degrees of article.

The hours have been spent to
wait upon the hand. By foot they come back

to find position splayed.
Blanket having slipped
passive voicing overnight get up
into that high-end realness hiss

against nature and poetry

not to love
what found out
side to air

from here and
it is mine.
They are not
those many who

And you bend
cough loop down
into your chest
species of embroidery

pocketing the different
crest of eucalyptus
public waterworks maintain.

The ends alternate,
unless to give instruction were
the ugly truth a makeup line
lifted off in caustic water

86'ed those years

Constituent Assembly
rosy American fetish
now regress by mouth

to the new
transitional object
for object-rule no white spray-plume
is oceanic feeling 'bout the whole damn world

discrepancy so as to click past
called filtration sucks wet lint from
chemical soup and candidate pool

The regularity of accidents becomes a thing to notice once a sense of interval has been established. This is what one finds gouged into the gates of the new hell, which is an ellipse so as to look like the back of your own head suspended before you in a double mirror. All you cannot see is the step you take to enter, the cupped hand that, bringing pooled milk to the mouth delivers dirty salt from the flats in its place. Walk past your eyes now and you'll grow feelers through which to strain to be a more sensitive instrument, registering the reduction of all things to everything. The goal here, as always, is to enumerate the bubbles of nitrogen rising in your blood, their fractionally unimportant shades of difference, before they do the same to you. Nothing surprises in the codes of dense chromaticism, and the reflecting pond sticks wetly to the air.

Counting the Hours Up to One

To take dictation light,
no sugar. On the wet café table
words lift off paper. "I got touched,"

they say, as if this would be the heads-up

former associates in the life were
looking for. State's take-charge guy walks and talks
in Oakland. How your smarting grievance,
smacked across the lips by the same dawn every time,
is a fully justified text,
needful to boot, and still
beside the point. One remembers a wave
and a hovering gull. They were emblems for

an unemployment crisis, and chafed
genital flesh. When was it they moved out
for the afterlife of all you thought well-broken?

            And another thing…

                        But seriously, we made it up.
Gulled by the wave of applause
anonymous hand on delayed platform

boots up the commuter, or puts a foot down.

Assured of our salvation, the loud exhaust fan
till the spit flies and feathers ring the mouth
in gain that boosted turkey shoots to get you ill.
Dumb grief makes a crappy hortatory balcony.
The real live boy policy has cut the strings
they pull back in. Or drag into the back.
Then, happy drownings! All remaining land is
harvest now for "new sugar." Who'd rain on

full-dress parade employment for the locals
when they come so cheap? You're the softest touch.

I've been meaning to tell you
or ask you, rather, to tell me what it means.
Doled into your hand in Birmingham
is my character, name of Broken John.
Pleased to meet him is a mask to walk and talk
in Oakland. This is my theory

of the active reader, and it is dense,
both sticky and abrasive. It was the oil

after all. Now smack lips in the real.
Waiting for the train he would recall that
it was only Ahab, a.k.a. Da Boss, proposing
an unmasking. Strike through, a.k.a. tap the chthonic sump
or flock, lifted off like paper

building monuments in flat brass.

              They decorate the drain.

              My hair is very electric here.
I've been drinking straight from the barrel,
resting in the shade of a commemorative plaque
to flush the impure trade regime from new sugar.
Beyond emetic spill nostalgia's coast holds water
only in the breach. Someone's got it all ass-backward.

A good beginning sinks the floating factory to end
indifferent as to middles. Crap construction in balcony collapse,
so boost what's in the shot till it's determined.

Necessity is where you pry apart blocks for breathing room
it wouldn't all flow through. There's a reservoir
for ink or oil to stain the non-disclosure document
as it puts a foot down for you. That's the boot-up checklist:
unless you grasped fantastic names in Jasper, Alabama

there was nothing in this place. Noise is such a fluid.

                                        But you knew that,
and it didn't help the shape come clear.
The work farm came to ditch the CO camp

in the funny papers' migratory flock of

territorial saturations. Oxygen-poor clay closes
cash-cropped accounts beside the point. Barred remembrance,
so glad you graduated live without a record

it shot ahead to frames without a spot

to draw investment by the strings attached. Speaking
of liquidated lives, their assets of association
kicked off the train to stand another round,
Broken John understudies you. Not to understand
this lashes you to windward of the bank whose lobby comes forward
here to meet you by the jammed revolving door.

                                Or somebody did.
This bit of dialogue had to be rewound
a thousand times. Rebar shrieked in the gale of

put-downs lifting your boots up off

the ground. Gravity's the spot rate of what's
nailed to the mast. And dragging that harbor sure
can take you back, right? The needful space is yours.
When you stuff it full I'll end up nowhere
but right here, doggedly humping my state mattress.
So, smart guy, who'd go looking for this grief? Margin
of the save, of savings, of an eyeball full of truck exhaust.
Riffling or rifling through pronominal travelogues
to trade your impure sugar for the new regime flushed

through prison walls an indoor-outdoor drive train.
Muddled as it was, you had it down. You belt it out,

a real number on your signature song,
because the one you don't hear coming has
your name in its grooves. Work debars yard from cell,

a study funded by Broken John. All these
treasures — oily documents unsourced but for
forensic spin, bust of Ahab to boss the desk,
sucks, blows of telematic fate — were acquired
in a manner that has no future. Bindings justified text
with title "Ways of Man." Dictation is
this form. Its slowly dawning smack across the facing page
is killer froth where wings take dream.

In the theory-death of Oakland estuarial silt
powers up a tide to scrub the vomit. First things
first, no more options. Paperless migration's penetrating

cry of infrastructure forges on. Then, nothing to say,
or the reverse. The form would be this clarity,

                    plus or minus a few awkward steps.
Your sweaty back approaching outskirts of itself
as the middle spread by right-to-work
flushed a sugar shack regime right through the trades.
Current events have hustled me drunk from the station bar.
Transactional flow, gifted with the deep image of
a federal reservoir, rhymes the red emergency cord
with the 2-for-1 drinks. Landscape craps out from my balcony.
But enough about me. You were saying, as the sun dispersed you,
"a general slackening of effort as payoff." Good luck with that.
And one more Wild Turkey shot for consoles' ill-gotten gain.

To orient yourself by the old colonial map
breached the *cordon sanitaire*. Now run the ribbon back.
It's indexed to a richer loam whose alligator
boot lifts a put-down up to smite your funky butt.
This record loops a shoutout to your shut-in wilds,
freaked beneath the gilded dome, like clerks.

And then you're out of it,
through the straits at least. Had you read the charts
you'd know if this meant open water or a shallow bay.

All that's evident here is the armed lecturer
spreading chemically enriched loam around an index fund
of democratic lusts to cultivate

a city council. Calls them farms on the colonial map, unreconstructed
physiocrat that he is. Shipping lanes bear the legend of incident.

The exit into history, voice-printed for your solitary use,
is to hustle up from currents whose drunk event planning

came ashore and ate your little dog.

The fog's too thick for that. No telling if the tide runs out

of hydrocarbon haze. Runs into noctilucent clouds:

> which was all along the light
> to mark the passage. *Paysage*

and there is less to flesh the idiot genitive
than whom there is no greater loss in a pen for replacement pets.
One grafts relation to the hinterland like this
(pointing), and this painting, printing. Exit the battalion of voice
as policy. Real live boys display slack string
by the oozing side of a civil interim.
You bound up each such eye with gore-tex,
saying: "Feathered hair, a trail of spit from hand to mouth,
cultures lust for the domestic. But ah, to be a real mountaineer,
you know, with boots and standing up!"

And as you rap my knuckles with some vague rifle butt
of sugar stretching for solution on the wet table,
I hold none of it against you, and love you all the same

> for a small man with long arms
> is what to call that reach the tower

crystal cysted pre-instrumental sailing blind

to contour map a fund of campaign routes
for the choir loft. I was drunk in each
event of song in which you gave a raucous hand

to my first step off the table. The ground alone makes value
an issue of extraction from that blurred double take. We're not
a microcosm, just broken down coincident with colonizing cities
to take the view that takes an earthwork in hand

as index of each chemical rubbed off loam in the coastal reach.
The blunt force trauma you instruct recalls
honey in those depths unstirred poured out

a field magnetic with a vertical of threat.

> Some overreaching is to be expected
> where the clerk of court freaks out
>
> into the sealed transcript.

From put down to booted out it goes
foreshortening the overland route
to ribbons. They prize what cordoned off

backstory from the uncondonable back lot squat.
The shot that disconsoles it took an overrun at cost
and the world's most horrifying pair of trashed trailers
to ascertain its depth in lateral transaction where the zero carries on.
In centuries between two palming hands

that desperation would have traded sugar for the shack itself
and spread out thick along the passing lane.
Terror sweat soaks a skirt to brake your pumping leg.

> But don't strain yourself
until the runoff comes out clean. The shape
was slowing traffic in the background all along.
My fingers were a twisted mess

and the indictments doubled back, lost in the storm,
folded like cereal monopolies nailed by the masthead
to the question, "How much of this slop is people?"
(The answer: My eyes are frosted over. Boil water
and bring clean towels). It's all you can't see from here.

To make examples from decay of airborne toxins
in that interim of ooze became a civics lesson in how mass
becomes a one, and then a single unit dwelling in
fact is theory: Um Qasr's harbor in the Oakland estuary.
We might have lived that life cornered in the round
had the wildlife not resembled roadkill. And so you're left with this

penultimate shudder past the presidential archive's honor guard
to meet the jammed revolver of another person's fate.

To achieve a gesture whose grace will only freeze
is your own effluent body's limit on the road in bad weather.

As it were structural steel post-outsource, and *it*
were, you declared it at the border: that *on us*
Texas can come as soon as Pompeii
and more slyly. Those trucks carried out the zero
for the negative return of a republic well apart,

which image oversaw your dream-work from day one. *Fellas? Yeah!*
Where the party at? Right here under your shoes,
sociably cracked in the extractive heat. You can water
details of the Alien Tort Claims Act, or seek reward

behind the yellow tape. In default of credit thus advanced your
bootless sense: not regret, but soon asleep, as one "puts down" a child.
That plus permanent Grenada blackouts' worth of skeptic hip
will score you sinecures for pissing in the jury pool.
We danced so long that even lack of bullets pushed a lump of beat.

I used to think that this would be a philosophical lyric abstraction
– something about space, y'know? – but then I saw where you
put the infused vodka bar and damn, I missed the whole beginning.
I mean, this huge fucking spike of rock just rams up through your
smoothed-out concrete floor, and suddenly all the broadcasts are call-
ing you a geologist on top of everything else? The only good ending
would have been if Virgil came back to say, "Uhhh, dude? You seri-
ously left your keys at my place." And that's before the casting couch
got down to brass casters. Or burned down, I wasn't paying much
attention by then, some kind of snappy endtimes sequence stumping
for more in pre-production. The cameras turned out to be too heavy
to move – of course! – but hey!, the sound! No, not the tempo, just
listen to that imaging. 'Cause you know the architecture, right? Well,
it's pointing at you behind your back, laughing its ass off.

First, you have to control your thumb, for only then can you control the buzzer. So it was written and so the wait staff stuck it in your mouth, urging you to bite down when you were feeling rushed, jump on if you're feeling froggy. Stuff like this has always fallen under the heading of exercise on a secret mission to nowhere with a button – or buttons, nacreous glints of decorative resistance following the line of workout sweat down your sternum – and an explosive packet of biomass with assorted jellies. Trying to be that guy turned out to be a sticky wicket for the rounders-addled yank on the kinky causal chain. Now fresh bronze can freeze your face that way, exactly what the filmstrip said. When you cough you do it behind your hand but well ahead of manufacture's turnover. Yes it was the same thing then, always speeding toward pastry wrapped in crepe.

Means to map alternate ends in series:

windshield wiper scored narratable face

might have been in metal planes
a little rain   a drift of digits
can unearth to prep the short
in my joy at being seen
would still be real cotton as to capital
wet among all fallen on

acting full-tilt   *extreme*
subject up for set-aside award
in overdrafted gadget

fingers pinch involuntary muscle code

add up one frame in twenty-four

tableaux the stammer host

While inverting ends of serial alternations
slaptongue the standstill

to splice odd snapshot into film
extralegal cardiac arrest in time
to render unto ancillaries unto architecture
custodial and swabbed
called yourself mopping up
the lean-to portico

correlative slave atavism in *progressive markets*
held incommunicado amnesiac *of course*
the charge punched up through slab

lost count of days without a drop

vehicle here stepped from into what

whose words crawl off like worms nightblind at day

SOON AS YOU ARE WELL

1. One

Only interesting moment that one guy

    who goes there multiple

    hold still like here's a roadmap
    to prove I love your hands on me
    up this here wall. It follows.
Clean up on aisle of old men's hedged bets
                             butt heads with blank what
                was green my lo-rise *aide memoire* my plasma

forced choice door you gotta *want*
in national steel or ecstatic hollowcore
                can't won't recall in detail job
                called service. I'll flutter there

if you'll just lie down. Let me walk on you

      — *pure imperative in shades* —

outside the ruined perspectival space
7:30 already throwing curves

in mirror glass vanished eye commands

here be USAID front-end loaders
heartstop service call for all aflutter

Horses will do it, if no one comes
to eat them first. Latch behind you the political
               who can, bank it: electric bleedout

               fibroid lobing in that absolute ear
to be in it for the long haul incremental
bird flight / forest / polyurea "maps" ferro-concrete to
prove it I am on your hands reprove

        my apposition territories
        to be many   money   for laundry

The delayed dead slap of flesh on flesh.
BUT / *it moves* / home plate camera / outside perspective
paged from Monsanto's ministerial portfolio
how morning yoga how transtopian red squirrel

away down the cutoff road. With pill subsidy
and his detailed move like a job with time

how old arms mill in the park

border fauna nesting crowd control sonics

             "like my guts snuck out through pores."
Asymptotic slough speed to not arrive uphill in time at paradox
    and set piece wall to follow
    us here gene-hoarding *o rich!*

promised strain through sub-national chainlink
no buzz it's just the time and set to vibrate
guy like me with only so much interest in it all

    come shudder down the road come
    tape delay in live flesh
        misfire through the working organism

        handoff / reproof / hurl tomato
        mouthward, fishy glint of the integument

        long past invention pays off incremental haulage
    for the belletristic clean room. Former ash
    now banked electrical potential. Burn out back
    into old-time agriculture / what volcanoes want /
bleed down Walgreen's sanitary aisle not "who can" /
        latching *disattend* / stamped out pure event of face in lunchbox
            firewall description from the lenstrance miss-a-beat

at whistle stop lips flutter false-fingered natural price,
says you. Go there. Says, "You, go there."
The eye is not a mirror. The eye is a command, like,
                    "you know, not always so distinct in life"

whose rattling bus window won't keep me awake
post-mortem shock and awe brand campaign
apposite to vivisect commission-sales territory war —

                    "On the stage," not "at this stage."
Lightly burned / contract fairy tale for the rest

                              or what's meant by wheeling rates
the pressure as "tremendous." It'll mess you up.
Now down to dry heave among the slobbering coyotes

their children will make license plates
        the sheer will to wallow:
                    "On the one," not "one on one"

big load of it for the end user / conflict Diamondvision

to people who relax loose-wristed walk
like knocking down a bullet with your forehead
while you exit in reverse to block the tracks
but "mouthy" as statement of fact?
That object falls and so do you. So do
your objections / crack sometimes over coffee
proof out of hand the embassy's reproof

                    those who *[as we say*

sounds hollow pluck from National Steel

        says just turn the water on

        and you can surely leave
        same old domain the cleanup edge
        one step ahead to the hole

every time "have a heart" meant servicing that flutter

on being escorted into curbside conference
not content-rich opposed to plaintext politics
in daily dance of subject and ruler. The usual solo.

This is the part where I confess to never
having had a single clear perception of it.
          "These kids, we fed them breakfast

and they come back and kill us"

would bruise at least the cop's foot before it gave

even if the hydrant goes on unaccompanied

foursquare aphoristic program each address
where neighborhood bleeds into the city lapped
unpatch in siding with the spraycan

icon painter fade a monstrance where the blood

               It was never, in that experience,
               necessary, even when sufficient.

The mark of where the mark's effaced was *work*,
the less hearing oral history for heat

strained to hear a substitute nation through galvanized chain
deposition to its feedback in public address

               word blight / the word blight / force
                         onto a safehouse on the lake
is caution-orange your eighteenth-floor aphasia your whole blood
intersection near the history of traffic lights in flood
               sever waist from waist to overwrite
               numbered by year a young friend fell.
Housing will not do. With nothing else forthcoming
wrote "not a streetcorner movement" no matter place we stood

was no topos but transit yogic breathing freeway fume and crosswalk

                    being shattered at thirty reassembled

                tag keyed in glass sanded down the avenue
Oakland ghosts the concrete
in the poem's thirty-five-year narrowband

                        or cut through what's unchanged
paper port's rich hoard with mulch of new genetics

        in the musculature of man inverted on a tree trunk
        back to stains in angles just won't wash
        slowed down in circuit with the mercury
        and lead. Advance plainsong echo
        a country blues for the void grain bin

He's quite literally dialectic on its head
transferred pill subsidy to patent holder still a cutoff

            which is almost all of it

        as gravity cold-stamped circular reasons

        are Buffalo bones in iron Tho' Dark
as cabinets waltz a line of succession through your head
tell a tale — of high-tension *habitus*

                        relaxing wrist on flicker-free small arms
                        passing down the ends of major conflict

free while the scripture farms a loan-strained mass
about your ears. About what you'd expect
wet depression from vistas not this relative leer
from what can't — stake 'em — handicraft drowntown
from writing waiting to be wounded

            Unthwarted Vichy gland of interregnum
            called over what keeps overing

committed territory to the war as a concerted apposition

                   the kids all drink to cure neuralgia.

The lips do move. But it is not a movement.
The rats have been poisoned,
the scale model has been built.

Signing documents between the high-yield rounds
to turn up at the phrase, "Dance, motherfucker,"

        tender inarticulate poke in eye
        from voice cracked, chafed in love
        wept, or smarted in his alkaloid breath
        from stomping ground below sea level
        I pass away to the performance

was meant for scarred shoulder blade no sharper than that
is a songbird breasting heatsink

            that contracted audient and obdurate
            private negative in basement corner

       porn, dissent, and online commerce

the money's body now by love possessed.

One-fifteen inside the house, mosquitoes, a wet hijab
made to seem vacation prose
hoofed narrative out of shuffled deck see

something to cry about raise something
      to see the different look
      up to bullet ping on tin roof —
You hoist a topsail of powdered earth
disburse the fake address

dull symptom aching yeast the air
reads front page through plastic shield

just lodge calciferous pellet flesh
developing dependencies like salt and
Bremer to the blackout says, "Let's roll,"

a life of under-budget overtime
says honesty's the most important thing
in acting. One year late for new life
                                        a strand or two of hair escapes
scripted vision's conflict's end in diamond-hard load unborne
out of great need for greater.
A symptom slows, paid in notes to raise unfilled imperative
with social push to call you "dumbass" on the bus.
What doesn't break you palpitates the feeding tube
at which you realized the revelers were pissed.
And thus did conquest stoop to zoning
where ok I didn't have a grip I
watched the wage blow up. From anchored barge
free radical pus flows level from a relative commanding height
comes distraction from the drill team
whom well-armed malls unpack.
Advanced pearl of great price in prededucted uniform at
"this stage" not on forever aiming for
inverse fiat lux drawn rationalization budgets
all else submerged in fat, humid buzz.
That, and the fact that you're faking it
                                        to let it slide. Yesterday
                                        was a lazy, ugly time
                                        zone of scarcity
                                        tare of genitive

of genitive, as "Avanti!" irresolved into reaction.

Value added every point of nothing made. "Love you"

                        what the guy in hairnet
                        never said. Asked
                        for light, thick language medium
                        to drip. Concretion massing
                        up against *some* wall, to simplify

your head, weighted with the allergens of talk at
getting what I have, not what you want, sprees
have planned your end in the eternal.
And wet bees forecast weathered speech.

It squats on the tip of the tongue
cantilevered as the eastern elevated road
which similar almost is all of it in fact
stabilizing housefronts with ornamental trees'
unstoppered threat. Through the whole
                                        arrangement wind
        our parentage won't break the alias
        incomplete sentence got the world
        unrushed adjusting baud rates
        had out, in hand. Sweat-soaked smoke.
Whether or not sirens' Doppler shift is *place*,
        as if drama were to build a set
        at once in judgment in the fog
        the suck was almost not, not therapy.
                        Dry fuchsia clatter drop
                        the old shoe, sweet sigh
of pollen from magnolia and the bottlebrush as limit
through the change in what's uncut.
Exiting the Stockton-Sutter garage, seismically indeterminate
list of jobs you'll never have rams your image back.
Like me, a werewolf preparing for a run
for president, they self-medicate the 19th century
gone strategic under dark, hairy wood /
would not stand in streets. Write cornered
of my werewolf girlfriend, I thought it all
would be moony sex / *sum and remains the claw's*
bloody edge / fine line overlap our mutant cycles
without young speculators. Who'd the sump pump spit
into the dreamwork? Why not howl?
The larger animals go on standby in the lobby,
animatronic theme construction in the moment.
Despite that ragged flesh a civil discourse
now squandered coefficient of friction. Chillout
but a single day for neither to be human and consumed
sends along tricked form as notional tales

to make us prudent Calvinists, prophylactic lycanthropes
on address list deposits for the public feed in back
shown off as hairless parts that don't transform
how you internalize the power lines
as blank incomprehension of my flat tax plan
        at the no-man's land divides
        emergence from appointment

      onto one-way street no power grid
      was dust in the repurposed can
      to make round skin uneven allures
      flush milk into lake as clouds
      reflect the bottom up

           say I'm not here so call

soon as you've gone too
dead into new heart's double stroke
fuel of lymph and mucus in the exit
got this one on health department stairs
ascending abstinence ed's austerity largesse
is where the bus just blows by blows you know
because the worms is worms no matter what
      says where on the block you stand

        And here you are
        Curves the earth opposite

but potholes ripe for overflow stand out
as monumental crawling in to talk yourself up
      worried at identity that spotweld still aches
to wish that something touched through vellum or the snag
on underside of your tableau conversion into coin

     that what-you-will being precisely drive shaft

        metal adds sublimity to water.
        The hard chime is a soprano,
        reached up from limestone to the line
        right in the neck. Remaining block

is excess blood the eye siphoned
as wind that retrofitting
feels it ratchet in your joints
another day more glare.

Meanwhile, standing over ground
TVs, stereos, air conditioners circulate

even from the air in fallow field
to point out utile prime of newish colonies
limited by the coming agricultural collapse /
almost overnight a vast emporium of imported
glint off bright pyramidal soda cans blocked highway

of resistance? / *resistance is Stalinism!* / so will be
subject of "consensus" for (soon-to-be-named)

container full of bargain-basement Tyson legs
scanned as "bold yet risky economic strategy"
traffic calming conduit jammed up subsidy
as outflow draining off accumulation. Not mass input like
chicken farming, for example, at a loss
where devaluing devalued values in that "post-war" situation

become new languages of space in permanent fog.

Or over water,
sinking part way in

is oil a nictitating membrane
over clouded cornea no help

Voice in Senegalese French
says, "control," say "will not pass"

what it is we'd both rather not
now anonymous collateral stilling ripples

Figure of an outward discount
I'd prefer not to hear as reconstruction

                              in an Oakland English
                        scrying futures. Enunciate
                to seal disclosing archive waters
                neutral buoyancy in outflow lake
                strange aluminum paddle-wheel barge

                        makes it all the more lifelike
                        displacing effluent petroleum

                to babble you release the less-arrested wealth
                        but intuit othersided. Guns fire light.

                If unpublished, it's infinite attribution
                to whatever gesture money makes

                gum the structure from the drill rig
                out of pocket. Just do you to it

                uncamouflaged her voluble blanket fort his lead levels
                                        — that kind of prurient rotation.
                Void this follows transatlantic here up wall
                to bat the source around the ended inquiry
                why asphyxiated crescent moon why blue bullet
                                called resource trust fund called strike
                                marks up watermark effacing work.

                Shirt so bright it hurts on early train
                begged water at the gallery door

                                        liquidity event is eyes

                tearing up in glare investing glass.
                To your easy laugh at politics aforesaid
                smell of trash day in the heat wave

                To ask why people cut their limbs.
                To make a midden bloom in desert

                        fertilize the walk to work

only to a point. How else to be confirmed?
The sun is less ubiquitous than mirrors
                              pierced room of twenty-five sealed
or locked out in the run-up. The details are baroque, on

period instruments, hangover and transit slowdown
sights on monetizing street
while driving paper on the sidewalk.

Squinting at the export trade
business section wrapped around sports

its inmost heart. What but a plaint
thickened by the new green diesel
Mama may have his own

communities of interest. Average rate

mute participation to partition
a lengthening commute through forced glut.

Show us all self-understood as betting men
whose emergence into famine overstocks
red Toyota pickup unbound a moment from

the colonial cash transfer to balance payment.
Stalled train hums beside the shuttered yeast plant

     so you live to be a private utility monopoly
     awake and talking to the phone. Trampled
     poll's upside department holler steals a cut of

echoes. Not to correspond but match the speed
cornered skin-dust swapped in balanced lots
     of trees deep green in window wish you

          there between. A history together comes to fence

               old mill from armed park — however.

     Fruit of Islam reads The Final Call in next seat. Sleeper
off-record, from her signal loss outside a private tent city
              as years go by. Muttered data dump
       cantilevering the eastern roadbed into air
       sometimes folks around here breathe.

Reflected furlough face unphotographable

     but for algorithmic recognition metrics
     apposite at war with *territorial commitment*
"progressive" weekly's econ / *speedup for the social wage*

under which no town unwon
to collusion's ethical turn.
Unimproved in body but it melted

             sweetly on your tongue
             resequenced to grow hair

warns of sports-related nudity, crude situation language,
late returns / countervailing toll forward is
ambiguous at best per alto player over coffee. *Settle*
armed relax with flick of wrist a smaller time
pictures who on sidewalk you resemble how

short-term shelter filled your mouth
with the usual salts and silver.

Just think certain low hum how selected neighborhoods
      fire the soldier who mimicked speech
      killed / *everyone a cop, slobbering*

to ideology as the actual itself: what got done

called into responsibility by a four-color print job.

*D*ear *Else,*

I was scraping my foot along the all-purpose, landlord-gray carpet when your articulate admission came to keep time. You were arbitrary and inscrutable in the face of my complaint about the always-resurfaced road-bed of someone else's progress toward death. In that web your head would save my face as an icy filter for the excess skin flexing its curve into the apparatus in the boiler room. The question here, as always, was a lack of copula despite the many good words humming happily along their way to the pit of civil engineering they enter without limit but never seem to fill. Sixteen bodies grapple with the cauterized district bounding the crosscut parkways. But there you were still, prodding me with an unknown mass of hot air.

Love,
And Whatnot

The four-year-old shakes her dreads in the early brightness
            and I have to maybe take a break from this.

            To eat their politics first you throw the latch behind
who got did. Recall your co-worker hurled across the casket lid
faith into gut a missile for congratulations
did it and it's done, incontrovertible. That is
act as one life late in yearly news

                        to turn 'round bite you.

                But I see a fire,
        where they burned the ship they bombed
to park my cheapest car, young director from the avenues
                all over local color

                        unsure as to meaning but hypnosis
                        moved out here back in 1-A.

We film in balance held apart from human affairs
        so wasted in a safe place of their own

                sheer expense. What it takes to kill inside
the speculative hi-rise. *Here, on these rugged cliffs*
a dead accurate gape and idiom of village
on rubbery bags reeled out of razored skin.
Said same breath as box score said batting average
long enough for hot particles in the bilge.
                And I see the glass factory

                building broken shards of present time,
                hear a roof truss pop in stiff wind
                hauled back to dry dock late at night,
                with montage of farm and mine to prove
                the more return the more

the work to pressure wash away the earth.

She keeps the old-time voucher framed
                              to move back in
            not down into the dark but pumping up

erosive pits. Name it for the war it starts again.
Whatever value in the ground was liberated in the spillway to
know your neighborhood once under water

            took one long the other way

            cut hands to ribbons for the artisanal text.

Serving the needs of others is the only
legitimate business in the world today
            — A.P. Giannini, founder, Bank of America.
      What bubbled when you scraped the sandbox
                  is less than full interior security
                  timed pickup gun appreciating in the back

on every front. Rot of the comparative
                  two-mile road *triumphant*
                  on a mission up to Emeryville
            cost price in headless fermentarium
wordless for the morning organ trio. In digest form

confuse a circling truck on fire with freedom
to have been the inverse curve of ground rent

banks founder on the late returns. Engorged for one
or serving only need to others to legitimate

serving others to their only need:

                  way to run a light-rail system
shells the mansion more and more like fate

burned along the track in Richmond.
Consolation / what profit slash / and burn
sharp stick surprising universal self-defense

diamond in the oil / specific gravity
march along the line / *on time*
unload unclaimed container Oakland APL
and swamps, too, drained
small commodity squeezing out my tight, dry hole.

                    Frame as can't nobody tell me what
when the corpse holds value greater than the ground

          crouched naked in the sparse, dry grass
                    at least a look. Providential fact's
                    coal-burner curtain on the district edge

which fighting gets you railroad for a hundred years
                    inconsequential, but in the nicest way
                    a sidewalk blocks a flock of geese.

          Reduced deep space to reverb
          and a plaque — just for showing up

looks like shit still priceless
for a full year active duty on the cheap
terminal exception product spaces
into flight suit's catch pouch what

                              proportions what
to do. Mineral rights the toppled proxy vote
you claw it from in clumps,
          king of the arena hollowed out.
          They've given in. The green grass piles
up flinch at sharp reports
lifted on a day of broccoli and the treadmill.

He is an exorcist, employed by the state.
Like the very phrase "an American

rubber plantation outside the capital." Whatever
          is refuge hugs blood and lymph
          through dilated pores

        to see you hiding there my sweat my
sebum damp reality effect a brow
toiled to displace. Three quick intervals an hour
drains off as unreclaimed humidity

      returns discredit. This art
      to be entered by the barrier road
      subcutaneous country bug race.

Marching down the waxy line a revelation
that "a week is a very, very long time" is

          Tea for Two unfurling discourse.

On the metal staircase, red-orange

      shows through blue my foot
      scraped. Death is arbitrary, at least
      that has always been the main complaint.

      Skin webbed your head in saving face
        loom above the flexing reed an ice
        gone crosseyed in the filtered glare
          down mirrored boiler curve

      to drink off double image in the fluted glass.
To the question what's the good word lacked

copula to hum down in the housing. Sixteen words
no more than cauterized the grappling bodies
radial as a parkway plan. *The unknown, the goose*
        hot air cut with cold, cold fog

decorative buff how much blanks the numbered bill
appropriations where the action is where rust

was topical, a fume. Freeway yoga breathed across
the timing belt an intervention — out.

But flux improvisation gates non sequitur

still huddled under blanket through the snooze alarm
plasma memory to aid the low green rise of land.
        Frost iris cancel or the frame
            gone to stricture / form of oily rag
you're getting post-production on me phoning in

the cart to drag horsepower home against.

Pass sentence then as kernel of a pasted object class
position itched in sealed directories where
icon doormats hung to cover wall
descending still of gesture come to sound a thing

in comforting progress towards infinity
of loans. In the echoplex the beats

                overlap / not a word on detainees

            lengthening the shadow of the odds
            that markets aggregate an eschatology
            the future prismed into futures

can tell by your ZIP code you
self-act, with reason. What killed
                this man? Bare, bare fat
will cast your ballot in the bay. Scattershot

never promised garden rose in plural flowering
decision marketer from DARPA channeling Pascal:
"The payoff / he's assassinated / legitimate theory"
damped down cells to iterate new minimalism's debt
                and willingness to let prices seek
                    their own level head against the brick sublime.
                        Infinitely divisible as twinges
                        fray the separates to sputter edge on edge

out of this world catastrophe market

                        column after column graying set
                        end to end in all New Roman Times.

Fishing *to* cut bait, marine layer just a little lower, so

                              Harm me. Harm me
good and fine-grained. Survey the corn reserve.
Swathed in stripes career plucked eye
to target sector post-hit historicized as niche

                              display in something screamed.
                    "Brilliantly imaginative in places"
of an indiscreet and fascist youth. Honestly sorry for the former
decomposed organic hand unknowing jerks off what within the cloud
                    is form of tears in backward-facing seat

                    wear the wrist down over time
                    or at least a little jumpy hand in hair.

    Where the greasy prints showed up too well

    on me as plush of memory slept beside you clothed.

Gray light, too, for line drawing with a clotted pen

Flowers from the finger terrible, volute, chemical

  excuses every shrinking skin. Come back to me, come
to which terminal the pole grips cable elsewhere smoking
anthropoid grotesque these biped orchids block by block.

                    Corduroy pants all night without a touch
                    as the more prophetic lapse. A silverprint
                    retooled incognito hailing through the bathroom door
                    make this twist of tendons what is worked

                    to bone. An essence, immovable.

                    "You're not ready for what
                    we're selling." The holy family
                              bones up on odds

leaves a box of paperbacks on the stoop.

Rendering the blocked party in the block party

fizz of solvents etched a fragment hard

              specific / spirit boneless but a spine
on back steps poked around in case the neighbor smelled dead.

        "I read 'em once and then they go."
But love the sound they make while rolling over
wherein one bare shoulder / guarded glance to front
a thousand tiny classified ads. Turn, turn, and genuflect
to market, to market, expense of the boned.

In the west of an unhappy consciousness

hindsight distributes. Light, in a field of gags
glistening bare arm through the Kevlar
uphold. In my genome, ya piehole, push!
Here's urban infill, define it: "between a man and woman"

which sanctified profit of industry in unlanded land
          commensal dropping out escheat,
bargain farming. 'Nother ground control sonnet
but you'd rather surely not allnight it
          makes a waste case heave erect

whose steel plucks a sounding from the hollow nation.
Or they join as late trades occupy old names unimproved
"non-idiomatic" improv smoothout soft targeting the interest liable
        and center. Kids long since united
        private life in section the monopoly of used

self-lacerating laughter line by line rebounds the build
your tongue snaked around the tent stakes

      guiltless. Not the hoped-for walkoff
      short of the airless port. The tone's ransom

        as a line to cut the week in two

furrowed class collaborationist homunculus took to know
                 the fabulous exoticism of square one.
         As three chills drain / while my glass tense pleats
         ghosts rise to pave the clacking hills
and time runs out of bed. Sleepers now parallel
start in a tone of voice and go on from there,

                 forcing blight on the words for words
                 to remove the cathedral, assisted
                 that counter exactitude. Carried over,
                 error scores the second runner

stalled beside a yeasted hum. Shutters plant a train of iris
stumbling on the station names.

                 But through the tunnel seated, queasy
and the melody's a sucker's bet on a box full of head

                         right where you eat. Or forgot

                         position in the brain a clerisy

my pants of motive sociable the social stand-in
under mylar notebook decals twinkling
in an eye for mute detail. Window shop it
                 one bonus syllable at a time

consults the dictionary where your lips do move
or now foregone concluding generational commitment to
the one or so. Bleeding gums onto theology
in the question, "Whaddya know 'bout Oakland?" unanswered

smack between "blown up" and "enlarged"

                                 on a tear till 3am.
                 Particulars reel in the "best of" list
                 between joggers and sleepers in the park

unattested. To posit form, republic feeding back

pronounces on the diction / locale / pallet on your floor

reproduced line schemes lint a push ahead of broom
through intelligence that's way above our level
looks like you're walking easier. The leg wound
hauls off and pays an increment. Inventing the long past

three clicks from where you don't want to be,
loitering. So single top arousal of the satin rub
up pyramid of faces called patronage the mural
hazes petrochemical displaced a fluency addressing

friction in the middle voice no opt. No opt, at all.
Interest-bearing always being

mother of every insane form,
the yellow boot on car across the street

sangria on the outdoor table at dawn

an indirect link found last minute in the past

margin / those lapels downsize your head
when we think at all. Right now I only quiver
cutting through voluntary muscle to the plot
over crushed velvet of experimental puppy love.

As in "ah, there's affect," all up in polystyrene, benzene,
pinholed view connector road at cold comfort foot scale
with small change fill fictitious capital vacuum
a distinction between terms / firebomb or napalm

rationale for the uneven military investment
in "places such as Liberia," as opposed, you know,

to, you know. No? Word on that "such as" is

it packs a full interior and ample leg room in

surprisingly tight, low-profile frame

straight outta Compton / new OUSD wage schedule /
                don't think kids are going to go
            get a gun and shoot the president. That's
            ridiculously hard. *Feel me?*

Shape off the line ahead of form cuts down resistance
'bout to blow up here *for real* the blow
categorically a punchline. Hundreds of 'em,
flush. I have plenty of money myself I
will make decisions for the people.

        So you do this thing. Maybe
        you do it again. Again it is not

        a thing. It raises a knot

            your scalp feels

on the wall, where autotext recurs.

Blond cinderblock is what skin feels
when you run shirtless into
the house. The old house. Two histories,

                                unrelated
to a nub. On your face a sausage-size finger
falls. Mingled hairs on the greasy sham where
repeated pickup of the severed hands, credit cards
made it for myself out in the shed.

        Why is that your name?
In the tone of secret lore: "I would not be caught
sitting backwards on a bus in San Francisco.
That's just common damn sense." People just call it
something different, it's sad is all

            the same. The same
            repeated to

        secure a single episode

of clinical depression
the sticky street / sticky people
meeting where in case of earthquake

to comfort of coin between the second joints. The jolt
lays brick for new confessional polity packing
residue of talk past 15th / *casa, dinero* every sentence to
mean you never touch money of your own / the formula

means to float ignoring hands that flatten you on water.

Calling it an occupation it's

a living
will

or won't stop dream to say goodbye
leaving me to hose the blood

and then walk home
L.A. to Tampa smell of melancholy dense
around gold standards of the public water.

You come to feel after a delay with logic of its own
maximal contradiction per cubic foot. Hips counterswing to
the left at 16th. Muttering in motion
runs beyond results to talk through your face.
Do you know who I am?

I'm a doctor from Canada.
What you had for breakfast? No

one cares, and I'll take waffles.
The circus be unbroken, breaking

without bread gets in you nonetheless
from hot pile's concrete cap

the distance learning spreads. Dear diary,
tap tap, is this thing on? You'll never guess

where I'm talking to you from.

"People are dying" is an item for your full disclosure.
We've all moved in, world like a sleeper couch to
your surprise at *actually bumping flesh*
around the breathing tube drop quarter in and suck.

I'm eating through my online placard mug
decoder ring around wheat-pasted gut.

But ah, orality! Pick your way
through piles of filth along a dirty stream!

Totality into production line of shiny
opalescent plastic globules filled with soap, totally
into world you need right now, or needs you, fits
your autonomic hand recumbent on the sales rack.

Today I mention object permanence
but try regardless. End of the line

loops around to test emissions with proof.
Dead horse / lax grip / fingers, fingers everywhere
crash without burn explanatory nullity of "tribal war"
is theater in round figures labor as a special interest.

If I could moan I'd be a bio-contoured figurine
with my dying teeth. Like you it's not a thing to swallow

but roll around all day in sleepytime
lit by the fat, jaundiced moon.

Hot orange liquid, "a grand experiment in democracy,"
campfire made to serve as smelter. "Had any
good or bad experiences there?"
The body to its plane. Each intuits

malice in the apparatus
or scuff marks on the ball
will linger for a year. Sour

grape from spooked root is culture

by which the keyboard will destroy you
holding value of a mirror buried in the dirt.

That's what malls are for, and this one's me
begging to be sculpted, handled, poured and
propped by an uptick in copper salvage

taking a hit when the lights go out.

Oddly filtered sun — am I
doing that? I think I get your
bare-chested stance.

What I wonder: can simple breeze across nipples

save itself from the suit
for peace of the vanquished, painted flesh
language of December football, all else?
I mean to say you can't get there

just by pointing here the gesture

is if anything more abstract than words
when insistence makes it so / salty wave front
cooled in molds. Soft skin on a hard case
draining world metal from the .50 cal reserve.
That might be water, but in self-correcting terms.

The grain of sand edged
The pen brought down here, then here
determination to get across the street.

That's not hair, that's dirt. It'll
wash, described as a young man from Los Angeles

or anywhere with lights.
Once the beer runs out

without shielding for the sunk line

is a green heron / is the lake self-organized

To place his naked call to a woman in the dark
in Buffalo admits legitimate authority ain't us,
ice bucket rasp half-stepping border broadcast.
With the phone gone fully dead she'd

                    prefer to live directly on the lip.
                    Forward through the intersection sun
                              and it is not an ink

        On the sidewalk early Coltrane, flies, sodden
mop, woman in a denim mini, weak coffee
substituting money for a tendon-popping armature
in the metamorphic sex of junior beasts.

                          Working notes handed out

charge throughout an arc of manual clumps.

Ratio of slowdown: one washer out per two dropped in

means him, without a view. She speaks through tubes.
            Short burst for not as much to leave

                    blur around the stain before the mark
                    that looks a good bit more like land.

                    And through the interjection, too.
                    Nor is it money of account

                    pigeon feather dragging glass
                    an excuse to leave the desk again
            and again are interrupted by the guarantee of force

though I hear it drops off with age
and the buttocks ache with repeated lunge
toward the body's front side / object crouch

leaving a blank line for the landing to one side
write into progress quantum gulp and sputter.
              Milky light left, brittle dust right

          silt bottom I filter looking up at you

like a zipper down the sky. Balance of the double header

after Air Force flyby, the predicate to fade back in.

              At the freeze, sound begins from there.

          Through the numbered columns facts
inferred fee unlocked down regional causation widget
whose accidents mount faster to a subtotal
it is nonetheless and doubly right to dub a "hit me" here.
All twelve inches of the president, $39.99
wide bore opening a tab on rote airs
                              unit priced to move
the split infinitive from mass.
His articulated arms, crotch strapped and cinched
and a job on moving details of his time
as catchall for any death best unremarked

relaxing deaf to local time across the rusty void

on tip of candle flame to scope out cooler
makes the life much more like all of it.

Periodically terror of the packed

              conspiring ground collapses
              onto a canvas blank
              with conviction someone's
              making shit up.

                  Oh, the crowded humanism
                  running numbers for the paint!
This unfortunate pork loin, larder of the spoiling

straining up in prospect while the slave lays blocks
in a pyramidal composition. You can wear it on your head.
There is still that truth in lying not to babble.

"I now inform you that you are

too far from reality."

Apparently I'm picking fights.

*D*ear Otherwise,

That one guy with his autophagous theory of the whole would cut it out for the sake of a beloved name never to be uttered. It goes to show you limits of the multiple as you're set upright for the first time on the freshly artful ground of UN Plaza. Everything faces away from the street as if to become aisles full of beauty-college blank practice heads betting that no one will notice their difference from the old men who have been handed off behind a wall or hedge. A nearly national ecstasy of service jobs flutters around the "Detail Wanted" sign. If you'll just lie down there I can make the roadbed up around you. Imperative shades off into the pure hum of a self-pleasuring device already operative if still unbuilt. Perspective clenches down to ruin on the pelvic floor.

I am coming for you,
But Not Now

2. PHI

Ask me for the pitch, no politics,

something light about animals. And make it
mammals, reptiles would remind us
of an irreducible decisionism

        lurking in the boilerplate
        with dope-smoking rebel fighters

             clad in matted women's wigs

performing our conclusion that from here
a war makes other people weird from here it sits
in the center of what we see when we look
to each other in the spot where nerve blinds eye
your note sidewound, scaling under paper:
            "I think I'm skipping Buñuel,"

urgently a week ago. You were an hour away.

Not a semi-public triangle wedged into

        how film would handle the lack of benches here
        that we live a level up from parking
        I am there, for sure. The service call flutters

a history of wondering what we sound like
where mikes offer paper word for mere assent

one licensed blow-off at a time, with all-night buses.

        Bloody lip sez up against it now
        and gawks an hour at the crossing.
Claim-jumping eyes'll own full moon catch-pots
with prior recognition / footprint redux / Nikes / radio anklet.
        This commons in reducing to decide

         going for a drink instead
      every single voice its foray into

    AM radio between the horns and drums.
    The flatland habit calls everything else

    gets beveled to discourage sleep.
    Instead of going for a drink
    a trilled pneumatic hammer, suitably distant

    could surface. All floats a share
you nod, and the price per barrel takes you home
but blinks for moments at the tribute depot

    that can't strike coin. Hand-fed
    and oh kind friend, well ain't it hard

    larking in the bile / our plat /

to build a house in speculating ruin
glass-eyed command mirrors vanished
bagel crumbs between the bathroom tiles.
Will you buy, or only roll it on your tongue?

    Wells up in a bucket
    to money be many / be laundry

    be spent an hour really up the wall be
    spot rubbed from robot eye

in the zone between the drain and the annuity.
To me, amateur, belong holes in crooning, toll
to mark release from massing unreclaimed
bonded teeth note down reserves of time
while lids clenched out sun we drooled us in
or might a fare pay for word from here as sent

    our sense of place in bio-waste

begins the chest compressions? Clump off

salt gathered in a shirt fifty-five years late

how handled lack would bench the film
                              with no leak seen.
Closer to present is farther from full
so the same bill moves a multitude

              to drink instead of going
              with the heel of the hand
              locked against the bailout plot.

Gates through which the voice may only pass in penury,
othering a skin aerated on a rubber sheet
and zoned out *grandes dureés* from duty free
                    rinse, and choke it down.
                    In this detained mull I cajole a steam

stood us face down to plumb the gas vent

to be here loaded USA the endless ID front
was our cottage industry / small rain up shall

till the grinning mug puffed out of frame.

With a fifth camp for planned overflow
which prospers on the pledge to take in all

                              in those putative oceans
strain the chain with promise of sub-nation's link

and drown / or drown / and / or drown
clone jacked in noise. All infill moans at port
marinating in filtration ponds
transfer points to untranslated shift work

To answer force watch the hand juice up a little gall

where the trash fumes burn at midnight

trilled a hammered distance. Suitable pneuma

come down large, oily, and inert.
"By the time her image loaded she was dead." Its bright

lure as a onetime home of life remains
the text of a stump speech in all key states.
As analogy for blackout, new moon tonight

announced at top of notebook page
to your rhythm gig for the Anechoic Kid.

— *in what the lung you coextend coughed up*
in tune that jumped you in
to work because the founding voice counts time to
issue a retraction in the overdub

bought unguent off a creepy, screaming baby

is an undisclosed location

sinking fast / remainder due / dude
        we're seriously screwed
        pixels out of phase with screen
        stacked for burial in unison just breathe

a shadow-split difference, lamp from flare

bright boy flogs as Vietnamization for Iraq

drinking up the going, going, gone instead
of garlic sausage jammed in hard to muster
                onset / piecework / to furlough
hand into a hiring hall. I'm prognosticatin', Bonaparte, try
to keep it loose. Lyric pops enter without bid,

come armed with your domestic overstock

coldsore face inflates and sure

        you're standing on the midpoint of my step
into command. The eyeglass vanished but the mirror sites

speak a language of the cell-bound mystic:
"Buying. And selling. It's just that simple."

        Thus reduced, what more can I say
congealed the language into jaw-wired icons

                oscillating high-speed yak to solid state

of eye commandeered by glass to mirror varnish
with melt-away irregulars? Planet earth is taupe.
                Some undermind declaims op-ed.
                A little aimless ramblin', lots
                bound over to completion bond

        claim-checked annoy solid foment parts

and there's something you can do as nothing much.

How that squirrelly transport makes a morning
                        inquire historically within.
All hangs on the velocity of circulation
                but I can see your house from here
                and how extra-musical must it be!
Not whistling in the dark, but barking in English

                up palms falling under target practice

for big diamond end of conflict in a usage. Vision is a load.
It blends in with the castoff lycra thong found beside the park
our metaphors, hoo boy! Forewarned form / hierophant
                in survey grid for crackpot diatonic
disabled paper issue into overheat. Dunno 'bout that but
this busted-up old bone debunks the modern
lunge post-intention plays off income into lollards

on some ocean floor Nate asked as morning trivia
                        brought the hand to heel with
evidence. That tree was in Honduras, what it's worth, the barrel

melting down under anamorphic traffic cam at Franklin

and your reasons, illegitimate. This tool brained birds.

                    A response to absence
                    of nighttime bugs and consequence
                    inventing pile of wet, red dirt

              the backhoe builds from under
              slab as question for the vocal track.
              Could go potently to bottom
                    in this air. Grackles
          pick crackers out of plastic tray.
          Ratio of concussive force to scale
exchange rate / cash for sick day / reads The Militant in senior seats

heavy excess settled in a dull dream of light bent
woman shook under turquoise choker, dry skin
into bulk rate on flashing from the form

taxi, bus, and headphones cancel into pattern.
Fog shrouds light the same as concrete dust.

          Aerosolized nickel was and
probably remains a different matter,
another fare strike under never happen
is a negative municipal self-portrait

                    in phlegm and lithium grease

                    to seal a length of pipe. This is not
                    nesting in the termite hole.

Helps to know the tactical value of your block
through the bottom of a 40 / 1956 / shipping days

into whitish ring of context on the mouth
to accent bone of no reply. So we opted out
          piling on the flatbed truck to rattle

                    teem and clamor with all toxic comrades.

A glamour on the air is grit in every gulp
said with fist in palm to pump illogic up.
Like you, filed as exempt, we have this plan
relaxing people walking on your wrists
entitled / *why you got no teeth* / endzone dance
        Larkin up to Polk / orbit
around a simple contrariety popped gum
for oil slid home. From this empirical kiss
what we drove across the bridge to find.

Remember when we shotgunned hits on that incendiary roof?
As it relates to secret hatchways for live mammals
            all of Texas and Louisiana came here
carcerating pluralism's moment-form, stranded out in Livermore.
The studio lubed your smirk for the labor secretary
in this retail mob licking jobless dime
dropped asphalt difference between bump and scratch
        drinking up what's gone instead

to rescue manufacture from the hand itself
the hyperventilating prose that was his second love.

        And we sketch it in the mud with all the same
        mocked optimism as disaster headlines
        on a three-day-old paper folded unread
        on front steps. Something gnawed
        around a ragged leather upper
        to get it through your horny flesh.

You are deeply loved, deeply needed

        in a taut, distended gut. Deeply
        wounded in your dragging foot.

        Any way you make the cut
this lame-duck sovereign of ouch
on soft lips picked up the jack and dropped a spare
of what's at hand to wobble down the hill.

You be bottlecap, I'll be clod. I'm always clod.

                              You let my air out now.
Drunken quaver, loose plunger-muted nervelessness
screamed across the masthead
how to make a stand against the morning transit
              map a pebbly surface of events, flat.
              See me alter in the climate, itch
              in pinch-toed flesh squeezing out profession
         to balance viscera vacuum-packed in compass
where the pronouns mean to miss you but the bitter fluid
matches your specific gravity. Call it a motion study,
elated crib of armored comp exactingly trashed,
but if we swap it isn't toxic. Held your nose to sip
then blew chunks of neutral observation. Dry lipped security
for bridge contract padded in a standing order's magnitude,
              strain it through the mesh! Own up to rent-to-owns
I watched you chase into the bushes, vested in the beauty.
Newsprint mulch enriches the genetic text of hoard.
              Someone must be elbow-deep in smear and acetone
              or dog, stink of all this language on me, sit
                          and let me air out now.

In the throat and sinus, hum a scale of equally bad temper
with ear crushed on pillow not to listen
cross topography of freeway in a fume of breath
with short, electric strokes / leaves / plucked from hair.
              Or the crash blooms / born atomized
              trace the small ache back along the trunk line
              feedbagged producers of production
              are the first I've felt my heart all day.
              How to clean up after carnival
keeps the question if you have to ask it here.
And you were there, my head against your tender rib
swabbed internment off dispersed extraction gear
                          or standing water, unsound
                          through sewage that we sail.

With query whether finance fits the fungible organic
drink up the gone instead of going on
to feel the beat of blood along the silted-up canal
it follows: one more tiny room, camera ported over blank

adjusted by a cent or two makes right
but to sense the pressure prior to the quake
hum. The guy wires chimed between us

and slowly coalescing in a toroid shape at forty
you whip along on the neighbor kid's bike
toward your campsite. There are buried

stores of free trade Velcro sneakers,

depilatory creams, anti-surplus geothermics
shoved my wisdom teeth back in —
as in method, as in a mealy glade

things endure where you exposed yourself to woodchucks
or briefly, if it moves you is it money
is a posture, or a pasture, either way earnest unbelief, confess
you have to swim to sink.

The drowned man mutters "You ain't shit"
to no one but the difference tones
cloud up to beat the clock between your ears.
Tricked out lips and tongue to rotate

global struggle on a slab.
Listing: item #5 refunctions
voices of the dead.

They point and undercut their hands.

Packed a naked hemispheric ground with voids and turned
the facing back away. Idiot bulk stamps
the B-side into techno-pagan hand drums.

A burr, a clench, a lilt blows out the archive of your mouth
or was it some less sexual kind of count
that you found it unimproved and built a loft? Galvanized glare amps

the general buzz. Taste is free. Intention sets you back.
Thus your failure to identify with what you did

does the pastel tower now stand out

    mass through energy. You call it circular
breathing I say dust mask

        breathing

        under

    which we are
    a heatsink of our own inside
    the locked aluminum shed. Chickens

in the unzoned passthrough are not mascots for the fall line
as cotton fibers clog the cilia,
drop dividends down thirty years marked International Hotel.
Critical urbanisms of the dazzled squint
stretch another empty shirt across the pallet head.

        Does you to a turn
        to language

        in your innermost where everything's a picture
        of construction barons clicking "capture screen"

on the image of their own inconsequence of

which the language does not speak they are

        following the loss of breath into
        devotions to incarnate faith
        in opened guts of mute

      trueblood nomination is a press
      release into the inner light

conferred upon a ten-foot-square lean-to
and a thousand miles of new electric lines can't tell
how good the voices sound. It's all sentences and words.
And overturn. "When we see them here it's entertainment."

Consign N self-acting mule N drill
                                        press to operate
            corner on the matter marks a street to not *not* write
            the money spent *won back over and over* —
            risk a joke and drown. Nation-building to
            money laundering as mall music to the voice
screaming at itself in glass / vegetative gutted drag to hub
turned the cars by hand an instance of monopoly rent
like, do you really need to see the broadcast booth?
Simulating hunted ducks and bunnies in an astigmatic desert
refit the lingo capital for stranger odors on a train to
this (at hand, *whatever*) potentiality to scab for scrip.
Now I'm talking, right at you. I have this big device
                            on wet cement my reeling rote
where privacy packs on pounds of privatizing mass
hired hall for hired hand count's trial by prognosis.
I snarl in the mirror as I wipe it dry:
a face can stick like this. But it tics a touch at your loose hair.

*D*ear Unattended,

It is a process like laundry and one wishes it would go on without much input, while a cheap car burns into local color in the back yard. Balancing human smells with the weekend's waste labor holds a column of expenses well apart from what it takes simply to make it to the job next morning. I could speculate on how much detail would be killed from the balcony of a hi-rise zoned into the same coordinates, but it would only plan the reproduction to a second degree. It's blindingly hot out here, feeling it as a series of small stabs on skin abraded by a dull razor in the shower. You say it's a lonely, horrible place, and I say let's read those box scores tomorrow instead. Glass leaves the factory filled with so much light that the amplified perspective melts you down for scrap.

Rapturously bored,
Proportion

3. RESECT

(Cue the dancing man with hair extensions pasted in his cap).
Now a gout of flame as the market self-corrects
and now the welds and rivets are a test
(outside of poetry) I wish you'd pry my jaws apart.
Then you'd have a thing to see: the new face I
think more than one of us is gagging on
(cue red tag on an adjacent duplex)
cues the centrifuge / cues are calmatives
to do a body good, for good (cue the amber flood).

Like dust that used to blow from Africa, the general order
shelters us in place before the bulletin burns out,

lodged in my throat. At least the inquest says it's not imagined,
cut out of the wreck, carried home in cheesecloth, dropper-fed
whose noise is only heat expansion as the drama buckles down.

Last time I got smacked in the back of the head with a shovel

like this, it was nothing like this. (So much local color out in front)

a display face prompts muscle memory from down the block
where one has fled in panic. (The black hole sang bass).

Buckle on expansion of the noise both relative and absolute

(cue package redesign) for dammed and flooded valleys
where the faculty of judgment is empaneled in the dark.

The filament threads your eye. Every gland you own
dips blind items from the well fire. It was this ghost of chance
that scared the children in us, see-through hazarding a guess

that putting hands back in hauled out the twin you ate in utero
to be repatriated to the wild naked, pink, and raw. Such a mammal

would remind us reptiles of a named event through which
the carrier wave could pound us with its characterless hum.
That tears it. Next hour, rebroadcast cues the score

(cue the hack from the Hoover Institution)
to cue up thirty years untelling in the tone

of hireling expertise. I serve this to your face

wrapped in uncut wreckage. Get out the dropcloth.
A job is to be done and fluid spilled, soaking in the jobber's flood.

Clenched open I will unfold my scratch (cut to wound
sucking air from the warm room sound) to the colonial music trade
that brought me over water with a sliding scale of folky realness
defiling in the red. Surely every grandeur groans

for an orgy of quiet recollection. Absent measure is the missing foot.

Alright then, I'm a flavorist, adulterous (cue reducing indecision)
one part per million bloom of tongues. I murder with a spork

and sound escapes, I guess, because it's low enough (cue
the word "alleged" / *cue it* / cut) to babble with the general's pal.
Without the audio you really get that hiss when flesh breaks
floating up from the whistling man who's all you won't miss

in reptilian namelessness a tongued reminder of your mammal pelt.
And anyway, aren't reflections from the downtown glass

auto-graffiti? This withdrawal flogs an extra nipple's worth of graft

incurred from needling drag along a groove of absent stance.
One clogs — inhering — the crease in
double line delay under "welfare" the digestive chant
weighted down with the injection-molded trade of roughage,
theorizing from a hunch that someone looks a little off.

It's funny that the misty scrawl don't speak / no joke / (cue hoot)
that we live it up in levels and the cherry parking spot

what you came in modest scoops of gluten just to do

the layout on the war report / ten prescriptions / five TVs

and you'd split too. Funny but it's all a blur
receiving orders. Then our sticky knees evaded in the bed
and the cables sang tenor when the asthma took a break

deciding a reduction as tendential law across the commons.

To be new flesh. Did they get to you? It's just a rash.
A weird makeover. Purple word for artisans

clumping in our failure to consist. In this greenspace I can read
logos on the jets ascending. Shadow passed through
(thing morning) in a fuzz I can't bring on

a kind of post-apocalypse utopia deep down in traffic calming
for the package tour of floods. In the valley of design all one
(cue the housing market index) has to do to beat the heat
is mold that contour right. Public seating discipline funks upwind

'cause when you squint the bright field unifies.

When it really is today, no one makes a break for open water.
What I faked: the buildup, whether tartar or crescendo
blooms on the part of the tongue for a millionth murder
with a smile not for you below my paper hat, above the vest —

which prybar wrecked cognition's foolproof readout / nightly adios

is "highly mobile reskilled labor pool" housed in hostel.

Unit shape forecast over Section VIII reflux of slur

smeared state supervision over low-density resettlement
and the head fills up with light. "I deserve the view from here"
strokes a guilty automotive conscience, idling the boutique city's
delaminated threat. Or I waver. Wriggling around
is clipped convection off the frying vat from hot wind drying borders

to drink in commerce through the hedge instead of going on
as third term swelling in the teeth misrecognizes this

explosive decompression of "I kick yuh eye," outplaced by agency.

Beside the point it emphasized *that other thing* that
lived inside your mouth and stared at me,
angling off into the chamber. Bang, you're dead

wrong when it's a matter of the way another body faced
under heavy guard inside a frame of several months

that haunts you still. They haunt you still.

The months, I mean, we measure them in sand
(cue stock footage of the aqueduct) or cue the stock
whose ups and downs acquire detail from the necessary
poverty of yours, and a greater saturation of tone.
Your face I loved when drawn in shipping routes.
Now it's always someone else becoming evident.
The square hole in the center of each video still
in a series of eighty-three is evidence of knowledge
that it's all at once. Even numbers on the keypad stick.

4. WELL ALONE ENOUGH TO

Leave oily surface tension
Beached contort to slump
Glare's unmet recon always
Ruined given builder specs
Armed in country scarred
The shill runs country
Music on a long
Thin wire off meds

Combative boil off stammer
Drawn against a walker's
Line taps under fever
And the documentary bulge

Hired out service expert

Brought something forward brings
Home to selfsame bank

Light broke with struggle
Lifted lids hysteric we
Scour change through sand
Something bringing forward some
Developments drop sour pits
In stockroom mental no
Picture but the lion
Siphoned into rearview swerve
Spoken back of slap

Unsure heard voices hush

Downtime metropole string out

Awaited word just facts

The worm encountered eye

Then weeps damp crust

Glare always having met

Weight of metal beeped

Out of dark stacks

Way up to zero

Feedback in teeth bored

Into own sake collagen

Out of service hire

The risk of clothing

Scathing chill near innocent

Too much one speech

Accord clots up glib

Flubbed gravity erupted tense

Personae it's doled through

Not pigs' trough but

Nourished on blank cell

Packs down dam design

Retooling secret in reveal

Whined at watch unhanded

Point not to see

Lost track of time
Until you can attend
Remind a name which
Morning moon at zenith
Patting head packed in

Pools up near mouth

Clocked pastoral hub stall
At nape abstracting need
Spits public flux sump
Held your hair back
In sight of shock

Please to write soon

Some forwarding brought things
As you are well
This fixed to wall

5. STANDARDS OF ADDICTION EXCELLENCE

In here, a whole lot. And it is vacant,
zoned out. You move slowly not to be grasped.
One of them are you then. Grotesque shadow strobes
and early damp grows a structural crust.
Cotton, to baffle and enjoin the talky modern.

Touched, altered. A palace befalls the bullet in turn.

Across the street men and women smoke.
They make corrections where they fall: the aquifer
has run bone dry. The grass is smoking too.
Sure as shaken. Count amusements and the logarithm

rattles lushly from each crystal head inside a crate
with a flood of salient detail to design a dam.

To clamor in the dirt out front. Absent question which.
The reflex is as indicated, sine wave in your jaw ignored

that this is where our net loss shall have spired majestically
to say nothing of what's habitable. Brick of mostly air.

A circle dance of color on a field at night, or the inverse,

back-orders bent harvesters by pattern in the seed.

6. Distance Learning

public private packet

wall nor fence

fluid state reconcile

greased all cylinders

call you mediate

7. PALM TO PALM AS WHOLLY OWNED SUBSIDIARIES

Combust, as non-symbolic in a view from here

The throb of fresh investment in a limb you never felt

*D*ear Glare,

Petroleum effluents were babbling as a lifelike wealth of dolls on the shelf when the siren on the far side of the glass wall announced the day's next arrest, more or less. Take me back there and I will fire the gun with a light heart. I will unpublish the gesture, drill for gum in your pocket and locate our politics in the chewy specificity of what hot asphalt means to the leathery soles of our feet as we hop back to where we burned our shoes beside the barge canal. Camouflage does you to a prurient turn, upending the figurine to take down serial number and city of manufacture hot-stamped on its ass. It reflects a better light than you, this daze of transatlantic sources for body sculpting in a South Pacific free trade zone mocking your immobility even while adducing reasons for it, and we bullet that list alongside brick struck with an aluminum bat.

Bring the noise,
Signal

8. ALL THIS RAPID TRANSIT FORWARD

from where the word is mum/

9. At Last, A Fully Detailed Coastal Contour Map of the Earthly Paradise (Actual Size)

/bled/

ARE WE DEAD?

SHIPS FLAT

An afterlife in words or
the afterlife is words

Or after work we lift
our nets and snort
A gray man comes

uphill fist

full of headlines

in the heat a bundle

tied with twine so quiet

here you hear the slow
trash burn. Close the window. What
we drag in has its odor there

A wet sequence of coughs shakes hands with the irremissible situation of the alphabet physically redistributed each morning from now until the last time for which we plan as it bears down on us into a lengthening perspective of distance. Day was given to happen where we bought back what we had made in kind: crusted bottles, uncaptured fumes at the pump. Rain spun out a tired narrative of the half days for which we used to be paid in full. Now we are passive, we pass, and we pass the vistas of a surrender in which we are commanded to see ourselves if only once our belief in them should misfire. Our trial is a great, patient wobble in the satellite's orbit.

For the Archive

Everyone agrees on a swift transfer of

authority, and we pay diplomats
to fudge the meaning of "swift."
Balled up on itself on

the way to the Golden Lily day

reacts. Solute
in suddenness clouds

not blown or burned but tuned a step up to

frequencies of blue. Were you here
I'd tell you now beside the point clear
shadows meet inside your yawn, oh blinding!

                ✦

On a walking tour

Short-term paper homeward

for the crumbling outworks

The hip. Its amble

through neighborhoods far

as all hands batting eyes

Means clear / doesn't mean potable
And in increments

cancel difference tones. One note

bent, projects conventional power
against any public wall

of the monuments of South Florida

And cinderblock, stacked
without mortar. There is the form

of our argument,
sways from hands chapped

and clapping. Tonight we open
everywhere, the empty practice room.

These guys suck but let us play

through their gear, which might be good

for the full eighty minutes a horizon

forward into vacuum at the cardinal points.

Do they have those where you're from?

(and a note on construction:

so that no matter how you pick it up
the edges slice your fingers. Sedimentary aggregate

under my skin
down in the part that stays

raw and splayed
displaces gang from line

meaning materials churn in mutual suspicion / work
centripetal from rebar nests at corners

for ballast in the balance

of trade arrayed a crew
off book against the lading

blocks flash from single window three miles out

CLEARING THE FOREST
(for Laura Moriarty and Brent Cunningham)

I.

in a heap or cone

soft edges hard
fact of paint

alluvial spread choked
the shallow bay

once upon a time
were *many, many dots*

totaled to a fog

against your emblematic strip
mined ground not abstract
but brown-green figuration

flush with pitscape

II.

And calling it a forum

gesture spaces out belief

to reconcile *his obvious*
pleasure in having

made these things
salt pools of sharp generosity

This would have been a snooze
jumping ship in dream but she's

a film or residue of thought

Start at empire's chewy center
and eat a misremembered causeway out
colored in the line of each explosion

dross of address drops

OVERHEARING EMINENT DOMAIN

through a whole head a length of

leak. This is
my rifle. This

is me rifling
through my drawers.

Had the memory
been purged in time

of time there'd be no need for a debate

calling attention or not calling
attention to stay
or not stay on

bare board. Stand-up guy jumps lake.

       ◆

As a contract killer:

The hand is yours

that I can't move but am
moved by mine

to note them there

articulate the one big thing
at barrel bottom, flipping.
Stupid, stupid fish. You

never miss the water

you're so out of it
tops their asset column
to drive the wedge. Go
public on the clock.
Set your clothes back.

Smokes in Filtered Light

To do with what you will

a function scaled sideways
to the single cell

to be that time on

your side and the other

time inside

the barred frame fails

to hold you long
enough to be of use
to shoot the poor relation
punctual to puncture
wounds the ratio of which

To identify solely as a citizen is to be gathered up like loose meat in a scheme to turn a profit on production waste. The tomatoes settle during shipping so as to form a quantity of discourse or its carelessly flung punctuation, rather than the rounding-off of labor costs in small areas of downtime that makes a little room to breathe between the units. Methamphetamine adds amplitude to a standing wave of sprinklers standing their orders at attention up the desert hills. It was no country to roll a temblor down the alleys where exceptions congregate, bricking in the ruin of the extra-national. The sudden impact shall have called a halt, brought the ocean in to study us at home. Some of us have one side only there, publicizing rationales for words as troughs the bodies drop into, and then again to print it out in negative makes of it the prompt for a long, sad holler.

A Hand-rolled Theory of the Act

Or let it drop. Here you are

in my participant documentary.
I have behaved badly, I am sorry, I am saying

past your head in a montage of evidence.

And drop it, the distinction

as to persons we will never know

how that provision was invoked

exactly not. Just try finding out
is why I promise we will talk
off the record of the record of
our talk. Nobody knows the trouble
is that no one ever had:

"steps toward a poetics of distribution," e.g.,

> Where the citizens gather,
> they buy up meat. They purchase
>
> labor, quantities of tomatoes,
> settle payment for the discourse
>
> on method, on methamphetamine.
> On the amplitude of waves
>
> a temblor rolls across
>
> oceans so to study impact

on one side of each body only.
Where some of us are getting
word out gets words out
ahead of rationalization's crest,
fallen at the public trough.

CHOKING IN OAKLAND

for Terence Long

How do you not swing?
An almost perfect bond

unites the man with thousands
circling him. He joins them
watching him as on a screen

he watches life seep from

things watched. A watch

is not a clock. It holds
the wrist stiff, outside

the time in which a flick
or stroke would come in time.
The pigeon in the field knows
your eye is there. Doesn't care.

THE CHIN JUTS INTO MUSIC.

◆

Well, you think about the money and you stand very still.
And still the surfaces will not adhere

to the singular perception. Even
when true it was a thing to have
be false, that anything not

this would change it

for the better of the worst. Thumbed oil halos

side of touch screen for mistake,
the right of way gone wrong along the coast

recoups the studio's cost.

Citizen, you are extra. The catering
has been deducted from your check.

            ✦

(robot inaugural address)

California, you have a great ass. I will go there
and I will cut the waste. I owe no favors

to anyone at all. Consider this a divorce
if it happened, then I am sorry, but Mexico's
a place I try to shoot as often as I can

full of hardworking and exotic craftsmen. Stick

your finger there and bring it back to me

when I go there, anyone not working
will go home. I have no special interests
so I will be a champion of women. I married one

and we are all one, for me to tongue your ass.
I drive an immigrant myself, no problem
with the fag business, punishing the businessman enough.

✦

...as a slogan for political ontology

✦

Where some conical heaps collapse there
is one grain. Some grains return

to the tops of some heaps. I buy
cigarettes and jerky. Some heaps
collapse. Some grains return

the same

then do not collapse. A heap

in Texas or Virginia, of cows
or leaves, into which a man collapses
consuming it. They consume him.
A price collapse in Mesopotamian grain

heaps returns on him. A pile. This picture
is of me. I am outside, buying or collapsing in.

PLANH B

Is where I always want
To be a little dry

In cold sun feeling
Not a lot along
Anterior cingulate cortex

Where you are not or how

Signs along the road

Would have pointed to
The towns a million others

Might have lived in still but studied it

Got called survival value
And I'll write that down for now

    – being nothing personal,

    to use the inside voice: no dogs,
    some water damage. This is not

    the inside voice. Time to stand,
    if only the hands held no noise
    to parcel out the traffic in switchplates,

    architect's renderings, reboiled coffee into

    regions in a driven wedge of purely shaken ground.

    Remember what the special doctor said?
    Fled? Not far enough, uphill, again those hands

    like two shovels, digging, digging in… Don't.

    Really, really don't. The rule, touched, a puff of lime,

an identity campaign,

a priori orgasms, so there's no need
left in bright primaries. The molded grin squeaks

when mashed or thumped. You are here
made for the ease of your grip.
In 40-foot containers the elements came.

Small hands for the assembly, twelve hours
not so long in the scheme of things

when sixteen spans history.

Made it, neither frog nor duck nor puppy,

eyes anticipating patience
saying, "I'm the point through which

you pass," extruded hot for the cool kids' line –

occupying comp time.

But desire, of course. Sycamore leaves
on the way down pause to stick

to cheek, then chest, then sole.

The parking ticket envelope, true green.

Every shift, reaching in
to clear the jam, ten minutes
music of the chain, makes it sixty-nine

subtracting three for lunch.
But sufficient fingers wipe

the face dry, rub sticky juice to
shine the pant leg, for all that.
Punched key aligns with transit cost.

              With a time stamp

                 the gap in place
                 is mine. There ought to be a firm
                 line, but no one knows

where to put it. Go back
to my place, in the gap.
Ripe plums and almonds fall
immediately to hand
or this would be my hook.
The emotions do not work.

Cash on account in the flesh, on

their deathbeds we
get the ultimate gift. They watch
the train go round and round.
No one's ever bored.

Something heavy in a bag, hauled up from a hole on the end of a long hemp rope.... But the echo of "haul" in "hole" would seem to signal that the exertion of bringing the unknown to light was a known quantity already in the excavation of the scenario itself, and that the pricked tongue tells no tales unless to dart into wet crevices of the mouth housing it. "He is most himself when falling down," we say, not telling but tolling in a hollow baritone, or, "She is the face that does not so much cloud with angry blood as float atop it," and it's true that they do, both of them, like clockwork. Each body owns the task of vomiting itself into the postwar with every such receptive gesture, which of course is all the prevailing winds of grace and its supple mannerisms will allow, an intercession on behalf of negativity in which they both like clockwork. Consciousness is this quandary – or this quarry, again a hole. Meanwhile my throat swells with echoes of a pulpy mass the exclusion of whose proximate cause began this account, or began with this account, and then again,

the farmers' market discounts old machines.

Is where the atrium will go
refusal? A crank-handle flicker
answers that the view

of things reduced
to a lone horse in silhouette

driven forward by the back
spun landscape underfoot
knows exactly when it's being

looked at, and from where
you walk that's one foot

always on the ground and
sounds like sand in teeth

geared down to pass the sound of yes.

Like this rotoscope

the plaint that time was
we used to idle
in genial conclave

slackly eyeing things
than which we knew ourselves

to be more clever or at least
quicker on the draw
finishes the long view

of a global narrative arc
that carried it in circuit

skimming ground around the world
by returning to the spot
we hurled it from to suckerpunch us
senseless from behind.

◆

spinning gaps

◆

A silent sky today
rumbling plastic wheels
on dry, pebbled skin of things

take place too close
to be other than a wash

More than flat
is what
Flush / enharmonic natural

gas unsharped a social letter
drafted in one hand signing

on the other does not know
how otherwise the other half's
Bolivia screwed
tight to planes of war

Inside Out

shears in hand to think
for shopping every weekend
drainage clarified the rent

and pulled tendon for to stop
the rain to rinse cut stalks

depression mapped passing through
ruby throat in impossible
light stain spilled on lap

level to a permanent plateau
longhand alphabet's endearment

without the muffled voice
four fields underneath one house
is what you signed for life
is surety the tree in knots

UPSIDE THE SIDEWALK

About that chance encounter:
are we really looking
for response in the surrounding crash

of what the sheaf behind the music stand
proposed to raze the barn?

To remonstrate with
tomorrow, as it brings up grain
and grass of the familiar dead

is a propositional utopia
blowing hard to change the light

by which we read each other
in the dotted lines. Polemic was
the wrong-way reflex, pedal stuck,
broken talk across the rumble strip

as if the impact were reversed —

All the bodies shrink from here, carved in polished rice.
Or is that a squint at office space across the lake?
I came a deal of distance empty-handed in anticipation,

split up into persons, to discuss the traffic signals on the mound.

Too much white light for monologue beams the city where it lives.
Reflex affection skipped the private lift. The stairs sustain a nap
cropped down to roots by hidden teeth that used to cut
against the pursed lips of your sheepish, cheap sublime

or higher comedy to go before the board's hard fall
wheedling all you're meant to see once kicked upstairs

stretched out more to wake up less. Heads on desk display
the case to make against collisions in the packing list,
stuck-up en route to getting stuck up here.

THE DUST CLUSTERS

Look, here's a face, if

you lean in close you
can see congealed labor, plasma

knitting brows in concentration

that has decayed to fourteen hours' sleep.
In the folds and flaps it smells
like peanut oil inside the head this

is the image of an elbow joint
blocked by hair.

Not so much the getting wasted
as the waste you get. Being ill-disposed

to buildup's full, like time.

Around a Lipless Mouth

(for Rummy)

"Harder and behinder" got misread today

as cracks in the rictus, as yesterday too
listened for some such leak of fetid gas

to call this bloating hope. It's a tendril
of what's planted in capacious hollows

of a garden variety host cadaver
testing nutrient conditions

prior to the full cash crop to gird

the guts of fatalism for an endless
war to end all wars that ever end.
The question is why anyone still harvests
oracles of anything at all from
mold-bloom wafted off *that* farting stiff.

There Is a Sort of See-Through Moustache

(homosocial poem)

Because it was a slogan for the speed-up

Because the weight had settled in the angles
Where the bone plates met my lyrics wheezin'

Like a squeezebox just because I said so
And I say it one more time because nobody

Laughed at first now did you hear
The one about the girl who drained the fluid

From your brakes it held fast in her fist

No no it's not an affect I'm just saying I'm just
Sensitive about my mouth is all we're driving
Circles in the lines and lines and lines and
Lines to do those backflips in the stadium lot

brought out by the glare on chrome —

    Before I bought a car I thought

    there were essentially two
    types of people in my country:

    those who walk, and those who drive. I
    was of the former, feet on the ground.

    Greater intimacy with passing
    and parking has brought me
    to a further subdivision: doors

    that beep for closure, and those that shut
    with mute, factitious bangs. In the rearview
    I'm that guy. He rolls from bottom
    to a surly median to conclude

    his big American project.

To Be Low-Density Fieldwork

Thinking would run uphill

at least one way so contours nest
for nations that recede.

Think so, in ripples, or still hyacinth

that chokes the swale. This was
the return crossing, where they drank smoke
to an obscuring limit. Flatlanders blend
cleaning fluids in a thousand sheds.

Pores in a sprained body
are relief
of standing water.
I speak for the trees, for shade
zones out the mixed-use tract.

The hand shears away from drainage where it digs the worst of all that grounds it in invidious distinctions between soil and dirt. Enough acceleration was the argument for an enclosure of the coin laundry into which the gleaner would be made to toss her cut stalks, counting on their dense and unpredictable collisions to cast up the oracular good fortune that would lift the acreage out of hock. I'm trying here to draw a map of more than my depression: ruby stain that light becomes when hunted down late at night. That we have stalled at this expansive plateau might excuse the longhand, but not the long century it loops around. Once upon a time those fields came muffled in their few remaining palms, as the signature approached its zero in the house.

For two or several documentaries,

or rather, instead of being

indispensable, they would not

exist at all. The capacity to make
cuts on the fly not only

in camera, more than that,
between several distant sets, slices
any flesh whatever however

thin the tissue slide requires.
We were just standing over
there and he came up

and said, like, BOOM. Meanwhile life

scrabbles on among the prairie dogs and snakes.

PROJECTED ON A HANGING BEDSHEET
(for Tanya)

We would have a kind of

shimmer at the limit of our

frequencies between bands
of color. My hand sleeps

without vocabulary where
your hip pins it to
the floor. The sense that
you are there was always

strobed across
laced lashes. Now that cartoon rocket

scrubs the takeoff but the dark
dilates us to fling it up.

A Zombie Love Poem

Maculated disbelief

Reach for no relief from weather

He is not so much a liar
As the blemish dares a pin to prick

Touch his face touch
His face touch his
Face it smeared across
Your hands is only the account

What you look like
Spotted on the sky

A liberty so large will never
Finish being granted
Never start

❖

...or odds and ends

setting minimal conditions to see the air

and duck.

As the woods obscure data on the skin
and poke. It's a cell to be chiseled through

vernaculars that slip. Cut
thumb. And duck
the capital work
in which the members disagree on number

or a dozen just like you
or the tower light.

Marshal your self-defense
and set to work on that commission
looking up, the eyes, make a circle.

In the Figure of
(AEC @ Yoshi's, Corey Wilkes on trumpet)

It empties and inflates
to a second rhythm

lung in the head. The lips take
command to play and smack

the actual with its own
raised hands: c'mere.

Come on up here, see

eight fingers, two thumbs grow
webs, the crossing
two of each, lines, the node, drops

tone into space under mallets beating

down the passage. None of him is missed to miss him more.

WORLD SYSTEMS THEORY
(for Norma Cole)

The waiting. For a fourth
hubcap, or a trapezoid

piece of curtain
colored glass picked off a

sidewalk heap like your

crucial notice of
those dancing nuns. Probably

it was mercury or cotton
fiber in the air. It was you
who tracked the song there.

Where things come from, Bruges
or Manchester, but for me
from you, who told me so.

FOR A STRATEGIC PLAN IN PARALLAX

(paranoid labor)

Day. And chatter
of such. These charts

you'll flip for we've
yet to sound this good a phrase

clattering around the conference room

gone void up to the rafters or
the girders rather where
we stuff bodies in above
overdrafts on what's beneath contempt.

Panic science spirals
up from wrecked beverage carts.
You'd call it art, but flee
the inquiry (appreciative)
that picked you for the corpse

                …a rational fraction of well-main-
tained humiliation offered as proof of citizenship like the fingertip
severed in some goofy secret rite. A florid script wobbling along the
flesh to either side of the spinal column, involuted so that the parts of
the body available only to others are appealingly layered like an on-
ion. A trace of shine like a snail trail left by the tongue that dragged
itself along the paper's crease preparing it for non-archival uses. A
challenge worth three-quarters of a million dollars and the wrong
head on one's shoulders for rising to it. A pillar stamped on all its
surfaces with the most outrageous lies about the neighbors and their
odd refinements. A refinery, a republic, a public notice, obsolescing:

I explain why I hate our freedom.

If it needs a name let us
call it star-fisting. How much can you

hold and what to hold it with
to hold with it? "Grasping it" slips

into "getting it" like gloves if this

is true and this if true is true
because the kiss against it

archives through the full two ways at least
one in the chamber plumbing funds
of echo where the mouth shoots off
the leading edge, well then the other loops
around to crack your dome. Played
locale sends word out after you.

"To the Funland Station!"

Be sure to mispronounce it
if you can, display some chest hair.

If I can hardly move my lips
if you can grow it there then

and then again if I can move

my lips hard, like this equation
loses balance and my head drops

to no effect in lap of lux

eternal yield below the cost of occupation.
Because talk is always knotting eyes
make fractional curls atop the pulse,
the board game, Run and Cut,

where the lectern waits:

Stick it in my divot

I'll get it in the morning.
Then this my friend would be
scar tissue, not very mobile so

I pace the forum on a ridge

that bevels off
to either side

from underfoot.
There is that single line

to walk. It doesn't turn
your oratory out to face the senators,

and the skin is pitted with disuse.

"We Can Rebuild Him"

There, where the exposed gray matter
glistens, is the interface. Something reaches

on the way to grasp. One doctor
says he's here for kicks,

while the other thinks to help

by boosting outputs gauged
in characters per minute.
"Gab and flail while I jab you here."

Dividing the lion from the language

but lunging out in front becomes
surprise, fatal thought to read.
The cairn of other brains marked
trails off into the trepanned everyday.

Out of a Few Things Seen

(for Lee Bontecou)

is body flayed
from belt loop out

plucked tendons from

here sight climbs into leather
find the dark matter pushed out in

in heat the calorie the clouding

abscess in the axial fold
time together after which apologia
growl the tongue too thick for others

overbalance critical the point

down in pyramids each aisle

In the Unfinished Bathroom
for Tanya

by sluice of gray cold by
the open window by the stripping

wall down to lath and plaster

by the by to locate
or to the ablative

dust in the ablutions

washed smudge of locale
back across the back and buttocks
clenched almost blue and only shocked

hair clearing topsoil says hello stranger

pouring water from the bowl i'll be
your archaeology this morning

The negative command,

spill of light beneath reflection
and the getting dressed while fucking

are really all we have to hold

up prosthesis.
Of agency

or between the keys the floral spray

of darker hair on your bent elbow
drew me down into your shirt
in fine-line phosphors so

to speak. Something there is
coming to have been en route.
How big's a fragment. Puppetry's
criminal ad lib

lights lights in like eyes.

So your cells bloom and burgeon with it,
they are still cells, and the usual

tick marks crusting all the inner
surfaces won't fill or stretch.

I run on fumes today so much

like yesterday in this but that the water

was off-limits has risen in the pipes
of scary paranoid civil service
I always have to fantasize

when someone's looking and I can't go
all the way along you like quiet
side streets where escape can take
its time with us — dry leaves, crosscut pine.

Between Whom a Close Shave

Expansion just because today
breath is white and got no smoke

Ear where industry beats the heads

and an isolation razor dawns on brick
that is the only real window

Laps or lapses

from your hand a vacuum
achingly pulled to sunspot
from my thigh I am

in romance called
sensibilitated that is
to say split hair
Half wrecked

                           ✦

(excerpts from the interview:

All your sentences start
like, "Give me." Well, I know a secret

meaning of is is

that. Zap me while this
aluminum bed inverts,

if you'd like to see what I eat.

Runs across the deep shag rug
at the heart of radio silence are
thrust out, then? The intelligence was

what sold me. I mean I have
this frame and it goes deep
to yard waste. Together now
we could extract a plan.

Background chatter charts high to start the week. Remember the flipside, how it had to sound "good but not too good," like routine maintenance sex to make a bed of soothing reverb on which the phrasing of an ecstasy could get its brittle highs compressed enough for that year's distribution platform? The plates clatter in the drain rack and this is conference with an absent presence or at least a rounding off to same. Each body – all one of them – emptied of its girders makes room for a stuffing of the drafts that come in at the single-pane sash window, bringing word that others remain encamped in the surrounding crash. Such science is like the music appreciation of a good corpse, and was never one to flee, if also not the one to seek.

        As if to measure the smallest hint of costume, cash sticks to hot flesh. Really nice that you could be here, and that you wore the special shoes in all your gentle artistry. Let me bring you up to speed: we were breathing, then seeing to a checkered past colored in the grid of presence. The shortened week corresponded to a prize that would be won, and was, over and over in a locked groove spiraling twenty years back to find a tempo for experience that worked. That's where you came in, finding a seat beneath the bare bulb that swayed and lured our shadows into dancing with you. There's a climate of ambivalent sexual contact paper in the region far beyond the dark blue your illness makes of these bodies. Not the marble but the words, as they say and as they say them. A lingering halt pushed you onto the floor.

Displace by Degrees
(for David Buuck)

A jog around the pond did not talk
authentication in skirting glass.

Up in air one mouth-sealed mask

advertises struggle on the farm
enforcing fourteen-hour ping pong.
Gender had its coyly naked I-beam

where we hid. Acoustic tile
picks up static in void of yield:
vendors who depend on that fatigue,
tower modules oiled like capsules.

Enough cubed space and work comes home.
Meanwhile cured meat tastes impugned
where the stepdowns reproduce.

From a Handshake Deal
(NorCal humanism)

Where the morning news is always one bad smell

is universal history scaled to a bubble
that seals four blocks up there in Berkeley.

With the dense insistence that there's more

to know there is the stare into a mirror

that is not the bay. He is listening for meteorites.
They spring back from touch, light from fog remits
a slight depressive crater in public amenities.

Clublike anemones, and fellow-feeling to spare

as a shared life blooms blunt force in parking lots, the star

of our milieu flashed across the grocery workers' line.

Might This Benefit from Cutting?

We are huddled together downwind

Of our own effluents because yes

We've grown to be this big the ground
Gives out before the thousand ratios

Gear the grift to say the future blows
In forever everything I said regarding us was

Not about to be regarded in your face nor right

About now we sprawl out sullen in our lumps
And naked folds though it accrued

To these I take it back a bite in every mouth
Full name not mine raise marble in the meat of me

a scene here or there of soft power

Behind an outcropping shaped like something

in the brain that is not shaped like a human

in a chair is a human in a chair. What drew her

out across the lawn to be here out of wind? It is very like
a tiny mushroom in the shower drain not so
unlike striped plastic drawn across with acetone

and makeup. Mostly it is like. A second human,

that is the answer. That is, the answer not
the shape that was resembling here before

when things were ending. Cropping out. It's late.
The wind is in the eye. It disarranges eggs
and apples. One time she set the trash on fire.

Knocking Down a Candle

You can't really appreciate light

until you look down

upon a blackened city and your eyes

are automatically drawn
to the pinpoints of brightness provided
by generators…it looks like the heavens

have fallen and the stars are

wandering
the streets of Baghdad,
lost and

alone.

— from "Baghdad Burning," riverbendblog.blogspot.com, 11/18/03

From a love poem:

Until the details of the missing tin box

on the night table simply

give up, this is not the time

to be so well-dressed in mustard
black and burgundy, nor to be
collected. There are parts forgotten

sliding glibly under tongues like

black flesh of seals picked out
reflecting on the equally
black rocks.

When I finally leaned
back, my ear stayed wet.

To the oil light:

Emerge from the police report

announced as what bruises

finally sexed and weighed.

That the skin burns
nasal mucosa
to be paid in kind.

A hit or two

driving down the coast intensely
relaxed into second vinyl skin

the person worries a glazing outside
of grit-polished aerial bone.

THE EYE IS NOT AN ASSET

As kids, the threat of haunches

and a slightly sour smell.
And had this polity been ours?

Vast as the surrounding items
that qualified its minor interval
midway down the weekend blotter?

A permanent haze then, of live flesh
coupling with a rusted chassis

and shattered vacuum tube.
Among those hoots and campfires

given this material, imagination was

monumental violence, piling shards.

THERE

At 27th and Telegraph, a flag
in green and white puts misreading

squarely on the map. I am I

because the black and white knows
when its door-mounted spotlight freezes me

every hour on the hour that mine is
not the place thus named, and so I am
dispersed into a spread of jagged differences
indifferent to the blind glass confirming

my singular locale in what terrain

recalls by its refusal to reflect.
The city fathers us beyond that tree.

A Pause on the Walk

Wrapped around a snaking piece
of air, we can say with certainty

that the stain is not a sign.

Capillary action, and the folded seam
goes gray. Not yellow, yellow is not

a color but already blares
with the announcement. Privately
and singly in public talk of cumulating
hum in compact mass, we'll remember this

and having done it once, to a sheet
or to a shirt. *On the world*

at length, nipples dent the dirt.

How much can you scoop up before the bell rings to close the closeout? What I mean is that we're left holding not a bag, not even a few loose shirts that will turn out too tight when taken home, but a heap of curling strips on which a hand back in the stockroom has scribbled an invention and an inventory of what it is we'd like to see ourselves dolled up and duded out in, and that these will have to be redeemed for a permanent fluorescent flicker whose oscillations mark a middle that becomes a solid state. So "realizable surplus" remains both the energetic bound and the surveyed out-of-bounds for our take-a-village-leave-a-village economics. We beam up into that celestial light, hoping it might elect our rosy cheeks and only ours to endure a slap or two from last year's dueling glove. This too has been marked down to move. It promises a revolution in the time and space between the prematurely old wattles of our hovels and the gleaming port city down the road. Such an overturn, of course, has always been a decade or more out of date. We were dropped on our heads at birth, and have learned to hold that pose through eternities of shots. One in the chamber, locale cracks off the leading edge. Ouch, my heart, inoculated, mouthing merchandise beneath the coronary dome.

Is Held to Be a Hotel

A chirping high-
pitched monetary
roar. Centered

as the column is
an ornament to draw
the heated pool up

funnels of
a desiccant
firmament
meant other

wise knowledge coats
the surface of a dime
completely in space

that time unfinished.

Where the Line Hitches Up
for Kevin Killian

would be the sound of accents calling
from the opalescent lipgloss
on the cover. One bright spot thumbed

into the mapped muscle at
the center of the city
until you're home. Always was

this diffracting haze of gold or
sodium vapor in the fog
that pulses limbs of grid into
astonishing embodiment

around the intersection
where Blaser's poem woke. Neck
open to the medallion
is how you flash how much this
place is what you bring to light.

THE HORIZON CROSSES ITSELF

adornment on the teeth adoring
hinge oiled up to lobe
a ride on paper covered wind

each strand there's gravity one way
or the other gone to market
cult statuary in the center square

a plaza for disrobing to negotiate
a pull at cardinal points
was so the plan the program
one new orifice for every cobble

and a revel a
revolver neighborhood
stuck door to equal
equals thus

at mid-county

not sound but flex of voice
accumulate a minor crease
flattened into breakfast beer

for twenty-seven years a vision
of a bank on this spot clear
through cracks the fault named

around the town itself a seism
intentionally blank left
line of brim to shadow face mnemonic
mark tailed coin cup so what need's the

world now an empty plaza
what downtown brick hems in
what the feds will pay for
stand in council being one

decisionist halftone

so no pressure it
doesn't spray so much
as drool unrinsed film

helps fog in parks cling
to armpit stink lines
tie flecked flesh to typed
instances not drawn
cartoon but mugshot
mark as evident
smudged head and lift off

on thumb the dummy
makes policy mute
with shutter shut out
news to burn for heat

of the enemy's trunk

goes to show through ground
souped-up the emanations ooze
of Hearst reporters' image heist

damping down the sidewalk talk
wobbles on the body edge
gyrating on the lathe to thin

a mechanism and a problem
for remedial math for which
the money running out
into the street and screaming

screaming shit-smeared epithet
it seems this week much more
the paper gropes in crepuscule
of realness the symptom or the scab

and parts less often fossilized

where shave and photo reconstructs
oldest dead male *plods along*
totally unfazed to pedigree

of half a billion years for talk
radio brownshirt one column
over two-tenths of an inch

the copulatory organ is
large and stout and ah
we are confirmed in property
inheritance a planetary scale

scavenged all the tiny fishes
for a hoard the primitive
accumulation of anxiety sums us
buddy to spare parts of hung shrimp

                              From the grainy beard a face
like mine only grows in ersatz patches, the monetary center of the
valley receives my weather to reappear abstracted as commitment
where I scan the barcodes. That column, heated up to rise from the
denuded plain, is the kind of ornament to do a body as performance
as the dancing dancer flies apart at the extremities. I'm putting you
on notice with this: funneled down to desiccated others, all that flux

decides. Infinite possibilities can stop on a dime on the dollar and
still knowledge holds them rightly infinite, wise to their completion.
If I look unfinished here, it's time to say that the lush complexes of
my flushed surface throb toward the drift of topsoil, and that a term
must come to the analogy to start,

e.g., the humidity control box

First to say that canvas
makes a hole and that
is war or otherwise the evidence

it is. Then the mouth is
to the teeth as the lima bean
to wings and mirror image fish.

Divided down the middle
there is perfect symmetry
on one side and on the other
there is one more perfect like a cone

spun through space that also spins.
A tree in space would grow
at angles to the conic sections as
to be the eye, a bone, is still
the middle coming late, as tail is to sail.

(for Lee Bontecou and Wendy Kramer)

AND OTHER VARIETIES OF PREDICTIVE MECHANISM

Might be something that you do
in a sticky heat, for cash. I think
you realize that being here

is really nice for me. See me
breathe out, I do. And something

shorts inside the correspondence.
Every day you have to seat
the bulb again. The contact point
for light gets tricky, like we start
from the ground state whenever
it is early, working on the illness.

Where they were playing marbles is
no word to reach us. Push on thing beneath
to halt any lingering of mail.

Spill some coffee on the blueprint.

Just to keep the job from killing you, which
it will do regardless in the end when
the kids outside unite to

skip the mediation table and go straight
for relief of chronic back pain,
you do others to preventive fencing

with a savage unsaved grace note
that routs mimesis through
the power grid, compensatory marionette
on a jag of spastic jigs.

Thirty-six to a room, put
some culture all up in 'em. Funds
for saws do not construct when past

tense renders lumber unto dust.

The Chronicle of Philanthropy

At any rate is how
you make the big bucks
stretch into the larger
novelty check on
pasteboard. It isn't only
contact improvisation,

it's also an entire
philosophy and way of
living with a purpose.

A starvation social
wage begrudged from surplus.
I only wish more youngsters

had this chance to learn to breathe.

Guns and Ammo

The sheer refusal of intent is
beautiful, and fast as hell. Notice
that your hands start picking up the pace

at home, hours off the line. This nation
language is like bees, loud and shiny
in the smoked air I sing through on my

own account. Business is the business,
giving it to the soft hinterlands.

Nine syllables, nine millimeters.
Or dress parade of onliest throng.

At the hard threshold cost is friction,
an impact study of the pinpoint
entry and the fist-sized hole behind.
Circulation falls back on metal.

                    ✦

The exposure is grainy and gray, an interface with light that had to
reach too far to find its object glistening in the frame of its subjection.
So no one really notices how the grasp has been doctored, purporting
to hold a pistol when in the original it was an open palm at the end
of a stiff arm, warding off the kick that, barely visible from the com-
position's edge, was easy enough to airbrush out. Thinking through
this is precisely no help at all. Character was the first output to boost
the levels on every minute nuance of belief (or disbelief, so long as it
too hurts) that jabs and flails at the viewer from those halftones. Li-
ons and tigers and bears, in a language hunting flesh, hunt jobs. Stop
reading the figure's thoughts and attend to the surprising cairn it's
just barely visible behind.

                    ✦

Now With Sole-Source Bidding!

The missing subject of today's bad news
stood smirking in the busted bus shelter,
miraculously unspattered. Some things are

just that insubstantial. Did this make the
situation worse? Well, yes. It will become
routine, an audit just like any other.

You ought to have been in these pictures

of an armored geek in spectacles,

gumming at the pissed-off and patented animals

while your name was quietly sliding down the list
along the axis of selection. Roman
Jakobson, meet Jackie Robinson
up in Boston for the bus to Basra.

IMAGE CAPTURE

Proving the delayed fraction of a bad end
like a dog, i.e., well-maintained and open
at the mouth to humiliations our own

flesh endures without a script,
sloughed off in wobbly piles of onionskin,

we trace the course of false events
across your tongue. "Prove it" was doomed

to be precisely wrong, the sort of challenge
three-quarters of a million dollars and a head

like Simon on his pillar could have stamped into the lie

of a republic that would post its notice
under no such mark. Now obsolesce.

            ✦

In the infinite cinema,

every Cretan liar is this one
baggy monster reading poems
in a hole as knots along a rope

that is a novel where *unknown unknowns*
yield to *the sharp dart of longing love*

floating to fluorescent lighting round the clock
that flickers on the clouded surface

of a postwar fog. The intercession of
his negative avowal saves coherence

in a theological quandary for consciousness
that tracks its moves across a field excluding it.
Public domain pulp toils back into print,
off the payroll. He is thus employed.

Sightlines Are Obstructed

Looking in the mirror
for your face when you
were standing there in light

behind my left shoulder,
I saw that I could not

see myself as standing
in or up for the out

of focus areas
crowded in that picture.

Some gravity warps light
around the bend. We are

stripping for the neighbor.

From the adjacent columns:

You are no clinician but you know
enough to place the perfect A-flat
drone of the larger sort of male toadfish

in today's flat file, thinking it might
serve you in another climate for an alibi.

What I mean is that
the poem thinks that it will sing

to you. Yesterday

Malalai Joya had a few choice words
for the constitutional convention. Rocks
thrown through display glass
at the shoddy merchandise, and here we are
doctoring the evidence to prove
a world that still addresses us.

The director, speaking as a private citizen:

I do not know you
but I know the chronicles
of your propinquity, your neoprene

and ruffles, outmoded mustache

a sign of sorts that I have read.
My scholarship, your history —
which you do not have

as it was written of you that it was over

and above your sending me
to study on the merits
of what you'd come to write
as captions in an album full of blanks
for you in swaddling clothes,
and expectably so.

DESCRIBING A CHOICE IN WEATHERS

But the last time I wrote
this book it was called
a sequel to the wet world

yesterday when day was given
twice as long to happen

in a space twice as broad
for spinning out in rain around

the passive voice. Now we are

undergoing with great
patience and ink runs
the show into the sequel trial.
The facts are wobbly as the sleep
in legs. *The mystery is that there
is something for us to stand on.*

F ace it, the valley throws up it own barricades having nothing to do with the boulevards that beard the *cardo et decumanus.* The plain is one extreme, a body under arms denuded of limbs that grid the field enclosures where it flies apart from them, thinking architecture as a drawing to converge on the extra-planetary retina. Our modernity might boil off in a cascade reaction were we to notice this dry mortar thud of impact. Let us admit, then, that we shall become or not become this mystery to the infinite that comes, the bald spot on the back of a head or mole on the bulge of a buttock that flirts from the wrong quarter of the glass, independent of our wisdom. Dig hard for home, freeholders!

THEY STORE IT UP
(slight return)

— notes around lines by George Oppen —

I think I can remember when the signature of the tactical used to spread by capillary action up and down the fibrous reliefs of whatever was left standing. In that variegated landscape were a few harsh, hidden declivities from which it still seemed possible to address the others who would abide with us in the strained time before or between wars. Now that interval itself becomes the open question. It is likely that this is the only opening left for us.

Thought in the temporarily choked and public streets, hand in hand in a human chain, can discern the shape, say, of an expanding series of accumulation crises in the progression from the first Gulf War, through the twelve years of tributary sanctions maintained by a murderous bombing campaign, to the abrupt shift from the tribute system to outright recolonization. What we point to there is a wall. The unveiled is obdurate in its blanketing command of the actual. No unmasking will suffice now to render its stones any less stony.

The words are not a picture of anything. We have spent the last century memorizing this lesson. Why now would we assume them to provide an accurate reflection of themselves? Who are we that we can be thus counted on to mark a place for the exemption, the exceptional instance? It is as if, faced with the total falsification of reality that can paint occupation as liberation, profiteering as the helping hand into modernity, and rationed food and fuel as rationalized economies, we have decided not to face what comes next — what has been coming next throughout "our own" modernity — namely the doubling of the ideological genitive, the falsification *of* reality manifest as the fundamental lie *within the actual*, by which the value of the existent trumps our project of the incomplete by leaving us standing.

And so we have set ourselves to build a language for this melancholy knowledge that will skirt the test of falsification, and thus occlude its confrontation with a world. It is not a knowledge. It is an open question, long deferred, whether is even a language.

I think there is no light in the world.

The empire trades under the flag of reconstruction. Founded on the abridgement of another historical project by that name, it is freighted with a burgeoning human cargo of dead labor which it must cast off at shortening intervals into the world, so as to echolocate by the thud of impact what it intuits to be out there, but which it is incapable of grasping directly. This is the lyricism of empire.

We had thought to bypass that circuit, flailing at the images in faster and finer strokes until our hands cramped and our breathing was overwhelmed by production waste. Maybe now, choking on that proxy dust, we might find an irritant to trigger memory. I said once that love is an irritant. I think I still believe that. I am trying to remember. When did we first forget that it was Ahab's injunction to strike through the mask, and that this was never more than command and control functionalized by inversion for the rank and file? After all the frenzied hammering, we find that we have provoked no response.

Unsure of its address, standing atop a heap of wreckage that its view cannot accommodate in the shape of a world it has refused in the making, unable to leverage this survival into witness through the carefully tended bog of an interior terra incognita: this is the condition from and back into which the poetry of the U.S. empire speaks. Whoever thinks to write the present in this locale is left first to produce articulation within a tremendous phatic chatter, the choice of sole remaining response simultaneously made by thousands of desperate isolates flocking from all directions.

Blank refusal was an option, and we continue in all our past tenses to have tried and tested it, each time as if it were the first and wholly unanticipated. My poems are as rotten with this bad faith as anyone's.

I think there is no light in the world / but the world. Always after the first. So one might come to the lyric as a daily practice, a testing over and over of the first world's evident "success" against its failure to have articulated an opening to the future.

One can only deny for so long (though this may be a much longer time than we are ready to endure) complicity with a world that knows it is one's own exact reflection, especially in those events in which one misses or averts the resemblance. Always after there is the sole remaining response, and the words must fill the space of complicit consonance so as to void it. The network's enclosed commons of communication is most us when we think to have turned our backs, shouting "here, here, here" into the unfenced void.

Lyric, because its fundamental is address to a world from a place within the world, and because neither of these can be known or given in advance. Without some authorizing cadence the clashing over-tones cannot resolve, and an angular space of blank incision opens us.

Anything but a "return to the lyric" – this is the cadence itself, whose recuperative translation from hazarded address to the metalanguages of settlement has *always* demanded such a pre-emptive return. To parlay the phatic gamble of the lyric into the general clamor and desperation of intra-Imperial counter-communication, is to build a language that does not return.

Something else is there, if only.

Its emptiness, reflected back on itself as an inequality, hollows out the contours of a space in which others might remain alive. This space, formed in the vacuole or gap in temporality that encloses lyric address, might be pried loose from the privileged exemption to history that it has too often claimed for itself, to become instead a locus for what is unresolved in historical progression, the wrenched standpoint of a contradiction.

(Place of birdsong in Dolphy's music, as an early field guide).

I think my poetry has arrived at a constricted moment where the lyric, far from returning, is finally *possible*. I think it is necessary to risk an inability to speak if I am to find whether anything can still be said.

On New Year's Eve a friend calls from the supermarket as from a general social collapse. "Here I am, and I think they will murder each other." The apocryphal stories of a flood of cell phone transmissions from the ruin of the World Trade Center made evident this latent suspicion, that all it remains to say is there at the beginning: "Here I am, find me."

Lyric becomes possible in this time without interval in which language undergoes a liquidation. When this happens to a language under threat of colonization, perhaps a locus can be made for the heroic. When it is a matter of a language of imperial command imploding with the weight of its accumulated dead matter, the opening made by the lyric is less than exemplary – compromised, clownish. But it is necessary.

It is necessary, and it has taken this long.

However oblique the angle, the poem's line passes through the space of a beloved. Why write if this is not so? The possibility that the beloved will not answer, is dead or absent, is interior to this address. It is the possibility that the poem takes place where space has vanished. The lyric is the recognition that one might not speak at all.

Still, I am in love and in the world. Neither is given in advance where what advances is the war.

I think there is no light in the world / but the world // And I think there is light.